DEAR BLACK GIRLS

DEAR BLACK GIRLS

How to Be True to You

A'JA WILSON

MOMENT
OF LIFT
BOOKS

FLATIRON
BOOKS
NEW YORK

www.flatironbooks.com

Chapter 1 was adapted from an earlier version of the essay
"Dear Black Girls," which was published in *The Players'
Tribune* in 2020.

Designed by Susan Walsh

All emojis designed by OpenMoji—the open-source emoji and icon
project. License: CC BY-SA 4.0

Library of Congress Cataloging-in-Publication Data

Names: Wilson, A'ja, 1996– author.
Title: Dear Black girls : how to be true to you / A'ja Wilson.
Description: First edition. | New York : Moment of Life Books,
    Flatiron Books [2024]
Identifiers: LCCN 2023037609 | ISBN 9781250290045 (hardcover) |
    ISBN 9781250290052 (ebook)
Subjects: LCSH: Wilson, A'ja, 1996– | African American young
    women. | Racism—United States. | Sexism—United States. |
    Success—United States.
Classification: LCC E185.86 .W55476 2024 | DDC 305.23089/
    96073—dc23/eng/20230913
LC record available at https://lccn.loc.gov/2023037609

Our books may be purchased in bulk for promotional, educational,
or business use. Please contact your local bookseller or the Macmillan
Corporate and Premium Sales Department at 1-800-221-7945, extension
5442, or by email at MacmillanSpecialMarkets@macmillan.com.

First Edition: 2024

10 9 8 7 6 5 4 3 2 1

This is for all the young Black girls out there who are living through the struggle right now, and for the strong women who helped me through mine.

(Grandma, I hope this book isn't just a bunch of "yackety-yack.")

CONTENTS

DEAR BLACK GIRLS

If you picked up this book looking for easy answers, I'm only going to disappoint you.

I don't *have* all the answers. As a matter of fact, this book is nothing but searching. It's the hopes and fears and dreams of an asthmatic, dyslexic, confused, goofy, introverted pastor's granddaughter from small-town South Carolina who was the ultimate late bloomer.

This is not a playbook. It's not a self-help book. It's not "10 Ways to Become a Girlboss" or "10 Ways to Become a Champion." If anything, it's just the diary of somebody out there who looks like you, saying: Hey, I *feel* you. I've been through it, too. I've been angry and humiliated and belittled and unheard. I've been down and depressed and lost at certain points in my life.

But you know what?

It didn't stop me. It didn't deter me. It didn't shut me up.

I've taken many losses in my life. But my voice is undefeated.

Yours,

Aja Wil

IT ALL STARTED WITH A BIRTHDAY PARTY

Dear Black Girls,

This one is for all the girls with an apostrophe in their names.

This is for all the girls who are labeled "too loud" and "too emotional."

This is for all the girls who are constantly asked, "*Oh*, what did you do with your hair? That's *new*."

This is for my Black girls.

Let me tell you a story, and maybe you can relate. It all started with a birthday party. (How come it feels like so much drama always happens at birthday parties?!?!)

I was in the fourth grade in Hopkins, South Carolina. A place where the Confederate flag was still seen around every corner. Hanging up in restaurants, front lawns, on bumper stickers—hell, they even flew it proudly over our State House at one point. It was just a *thing* you saw everywhere. And this was not ancient history, mind you. This was *2006*. The iPhone was coming out, and they were still flying a symbol of hate everywhere you looked down South.

When you're a kid, you don't really get it. The world is a friendly place, right? You take what people say at face value. Your friends are your friends. When you're young, you are who you are. You love what you love. People are just people. It's all good! Right?

Right?

I was always able to learn better in small classrooms, so my parents sent me to this private school called Heathwood Hall. It was probably 10 percent Black at the time, so most of my friends were white. Didn't think anything of it. We had our little crew that was inseparable. So then one of my friends' birthdays rolls around, and it was a whole thing at school. Everyone was like, "Ohmygod, did you hear about so-and-so's party? I'm so going!"

One day, out of the blue, so-and-so pulls me aside in the hallway, and she says, "Hey, you're coming to my party, right?"

And I'm like, "Yeah!"

She's like, "You know it's a sleepover, right?"

I'm like, "Yeah! I can't wait!"

Then she drops the bomb on me. She says, "Well, you might have to sleep outside."

And I'm like, "Outside? What are we talking about—*camping?* We going to the mountains? Do I need some cute hiking boots or something?"

And she's like, "No, the party's at my house. But the thing is . . . my dad doesn't really like Black people."

So . . .

I was just staring at her like . . . *huh?*

It was so matter of fact. It wasn't dramatic. It was just blunt.

It didn't seem real. I mean, this is my friend! This is my girl! It ain't nothing else! This was not some friend-of-a-friend situation. This was not some mean-girl-in-class situation. This was my true friend. We did almost everything together.

It was so sad but so important to learn that lesson at such a young age. Because it was the first time I realized: *Oh, OK, you're not just a girl. You're a Black girl. And some people don't like you because of that.*

I was crushed. It felt like I had aged ten years in that one moment. I went from this happy-go-lucky kid, trusting everybody, thinking the world had my back, to this adult who realized there was darkness in the world.

The worst part was going home and telling my parents what happened. Seeing the looks on their faces. I'd never seen them react like that. They were so hurt. So upset.

But my parents were great about it. Wait, what am I saying? Let me be real. My dad? He might've been pacing around saying, "Oh HELL no. These white folks are playing with *my* daughter? I'm gonna go down to that school and . . ."

He kind of snapped—I'm not gonna lie. And this is going to sound crazy to some people, but maybe some of you can relate.

My first reaction was to retreat within myself and not exactly *blame* myself for what happened, but I was actually most worried about making a big deal out of it and losing my friend.

I was like, "Please don't tell the school anything. Please don't tell the other parents. Don't embarrass me. Maybe she didn't mean it."

My mom always keeps it real with me. Her message was simple:

You are a Black girl in America. That's the reality. When you walk into a room, they're going to see you as Black before they see anything else. Not everything that glitters is gold, baby. Some people are going to smile right in your face and make you think they're your friend, and then talk about you behind your back. Some people are going to tell you straight to your face that they don't like you. And some people are truly going to love you no matter what. A'ja, we love you.

She gives it to me straight, always.

Then she said, "Forget about that stupid birthday party. Just keep being *you*—through and through."

For the first few weeks afterward? Honestly? It was so hard to keep being A'ja. Before the birthday party, I don't think I even knew that the cliché meant, "Just be yourself."

Who else would I be?

It never occurred to me that people would pretend to be something they weren't or pretend to like somebody when they don't. I was just always right there in the moment, with my friends, having fun. "A'ja" was what was in my mind and in my heart and all the things that I loved. That was what defined me, not the color of my skin. Until that birthday party came around, and my safe little bubble popped.

Eventually, the world steps in and reminds you: You have a body. You are Black. You are a woman. Whether you like it or not, that's the first thing people see.

Your mission, Black girls, is to accept that reality.

Don't look away from it.

Don't hide from it.

But you can accept this reality without letting it steal your joy. You can acknowledge it without losing your positivity and your kindness and your ambition. You don't have to let a cold world turn *you* cold.

No one's story is exactly the same. But every Black girl, at some point in her life, has her own version of The Birthday Party. As you get older, go to college, or start your first job, or you step into your first boardroom, you have more and more "Birthday Parties." Oh yes, you'll never stop having them.

No matter how well you think you know the game, there will always be those little moments when you are reminded about the way people see Black women in our society, and I can't lie to you—it will take your breath away every time.

That's why I'm writing this book. I know what it's like to feel like you've been swept under the rug. I know what it feels like to not be heard, not be seen, not be taken seriously.

And then when you finally *do* raise your voice . . . what do they call you?

"Loud."

"Angry."

"Difficult."

"Ghetto."

Sometimes, it feels like you can't win, right? Well, all I'm here to tell you is that I hear you. You are not alone, just know that.

I FEEL YOU.

The truth is, we're a double minority. It's like the world is constantly reminding us. . . .

You're a girl.

Oh! *And* you're a Black girl.

Alright, good luck!

When I was growing up, the hardest part for me was when I looked around, I didn't see any adult role models who looked like me. All my teachers—shout-out to them, most of you were amazing—were white. Well, except one. We had one Black female teacher in the entire school. I'll give you five seconds to guess what all the kids called her.

One . . .

Two . . .

Three . . .

"The *mean* one."

You got it. You already know the story. She was the *scary* one. Most of the kids and their parents had probably never even met the woman, but if her name was ever mentioned, it was always this passive-aggressive, "Ohhhhh, you don't wanna go to *that* class. That's an *awful* class. No, no, no. That teacher is a *handful*."

If they were talking about Mr. So-and-So, who had been there for over forty years, it was a whole different vibe. Now it was, "Oh, Mr. So-and-So is old school. He's a legend. Don't be talking back to him. He's tough, but he's fair."

It was an introduction to the way the world works for Black women. And let me tell you, it was a lesson that I never stopped learning, even when I went to play basketball at the University of South Carolina for the living legend Dawn Staley.

Now, Coach is like my second mom, so I'm going to be a little bit biased. Just a warning. I'm going to go off a bit here. But I feel like you already get the vibe of this book, right? I'm here to tell you nothing but the unapologetic truth—so . . . sorry, not sorry.

It seems like no matter how successful you are, or how strong, or how many lives you've changed, or how many banners you've got hanging. . . .

If you're a Black woman in this country, *especially* in the South?

It's always this vibe of, "I'm going to tell the *real* boss on you. Where's your manager? I want to speak to the manager's manager."

Of course, Coach Staley *is* the real boss. You're talking about a woman who won three Olympic gold medals for our country. You're talking about a six-time WNBA All-Star. You're talking about a Naismith winner as a player *and* a coach.

She's the ultimate boss.

And yet, I've still seen them pull that card on her, too. Nobody is exempt! When we won the NCAA Championship in 2017, you know what we heard almost immediately? Remember, we're talking about the first women's basketball championship in the state of South Carolina. We had all the pastors letting church out early on Sundays so people could come see us play. We packed out the arena every week for women's basketball. We put the university back on the map on a national stage. We had made the whole state proud. Right?

Right?

For some people, that wasn't what it was about. Do you know what they were saying—almost before we could even get the banner up in the rafters?

"Coach Staley doesn't recruit white players. What's her problem? Why doesn't she recruit our white girls?"

You had a team of twelve Black girls working their tails off. No, working their asses off. To achieve history. Under a Black female head coach. And it still felt like a significant part of our community didn't want to celebrate it fully. On social media, it was the worst. Pure hatred. Pure nonsense. But I don't know, maybe all that hate was coming from down the road at Mississippi State, because we sure did beat y'all a lot!!

Hey, I'm just keeping it unapologetic!

I warned you!

At the end of the day, Black girls all across the country need to hear the truth. I feel like we've been hearing a lot of half-truths these last few years. They're giving us a little taste. From the corporations, to the schools, to the sports leagues, to the politicians, to the shows we see on TV. We're getting the PG-13, corporate-approved version of The Racial Reckoning. They keep telling us they want everyone to have uncomfortable conversations, but then why does it all feel so comfortable?

As Black girls, we need to know what we're really in for. Most of the time, we don't even *get* "The Talk." The boys get that. They get told about how they're seen as a threat to police, about how to keep their heads down in certain neighborhoods, about how to navigate the world, about how to survive.

And that's very necessary. But what do the Black girls get?

(Crickets)

No really, I'll let you think. I'm sure the answer is different for everybody.

Sometimes, it feels like we are trotted out when it's convenient, especially on social media. I hate that we have to become a hashtag for society to be like, "Oh, we *love* our Black queens! *Yaasss!*"

No.

No. It's not good enough. We don't want to be some meme or whatever. We don't want to be the Angry Black Woman or the Aggressive Black Woman or the Sassy Black Woman or the Yaassss #BlackWomen! We just want to be *seen* as human beings in this world. We just want to be heard when we speak. We just want to be respected when we walk into a room.

We just want to be *us*. Is that too much to ask?

I don't want to have to be UNAPOLOGETIC for you to hear me.

I want to be able to whisper if I feel like it.

I want to be able to speak however I want to speak,

no matter what room I'm in, and not "like a white girl" or "like a Black girl" or "like a boss."

I want to just be a professional basketball player and not a Monthly Initiative.

I want to just do my *thing* on the court without being picked apart for the way I wear my hair that night.

I want to wear my nails how I want to wear my nails.

I want to ball out in my acrylics and not worry about looking too feminine, too masculine, too bougie, too ghetto, too this, too that.

And when I go home at night and I'm sprawled out in bed scrolling through my feed, pretending to go to sleep, I want to see faces that look like mine.

Where are all the big sponsors who supposedly love Black women?

Where are all the companies putting their money where their mouths are?

And where is the support from the guys? (The ones who do show us love—we see you. We see you, Kevin Durant. We see you, Steph Curry.)

Oh, I can hear the haters already. I know all their arguments like the back of my hand. They're always "disappointed" in me. They always want to "educate" me. So many people in America want to tell you, "Oh, all you need to do is just work hard and—*actually*—it's all an even playing field!"

Black girls, does it feel like an even playing field? You know what it is. You know how it feels. Talk to any fourteen-year-old Black girl, and you'll find out that she's got more real talk and common sense in her pinky finger than 90 percent of America.

The fact is, we still got a *long* way to go in this country. And that's alright to acknowledge. That's alright to tell our Black girls, who are just figuring out the way this world works, who are just experiencing their first Birthday Party situation. That's why I'm writing this. Consider it my unofficial version of The Talk.

If you want anything in this country, you have to speak up.

I *made* myself heard. For some reason, I just never "knew my place." When I was the number one college recruit in the country, I even made the ESPN camera crew come to my high school on my signing day just so I could put on my GAMECOCKS hat just like the boys do. And I *still* got pushback. "Well, the thing is . . ."

"We're not sure if we can get a crew out there on short notice. It might be complicated."

Nah. Y'all got Google Maps.

I didn't back down because I wanted all the little girls out there who loved basketball to be flipping channels and saying, "Oh. I see you."

To their credit, they got a crew down to South Carolina, and it was one of the best days of my life. (Thank you, ESPN. Y'all have grown a lot in the last ten years. You got a ways to go yet, but we see you!)

But here's the *thing*. Here's my final thing.

To all my Black girls out there . . .

If you remember one thing from this whole book, remember this:

You don't have to be a WNBA player or a politician or a celebrity to have an impact on someone else.

I remember when I was in the fifth grade, the year after that whole humiliating birthday party experience, I felt really alone. That whole year was pretty rough. I was self-conscious for the first time in my life. I got really quiet. I stopped looking forward to going to school. My friends didn't look like me. My teachers didn't look like me. But every day when I went to lunch, I used to get really excited standing in the line with my little plastic tray.

That was, like, the highlight of my day because I saw my favorite lunch lady.

She was the only person in the whole room who

looked like me. But it was deeper than that. She would always greet me with a warm smile and say, "Hey, A'ja, how you doing? You good? You want some mashed potatoes today?"

That was our little moment every afternoon. It was nothing major. But it was beautiful to me.

Hey, we're here. We're OK. I see you. I got you.

Keep on fighting, Black girls. Just keep being you—through and through.

I see you. I got you. This book is for you.

Sincerely,

Aja Wil~

P.S. This is my only contribution to The Talk.
If somebody asks you, "Can I touch your hair?"
The answer is no.
Helllllll *no.*

2

THE BEST GIFT A GIRL COULD ASK FOR

Dear Black Girls,

This one is for all the girls out there who are lost.

This is for all the girls out there who are confused.

This is for all the girls who are searching for their *WHY?*

One of the best ways you can find inspiration in your life is to look to your elders. As a wise man once said: Parents? They just don't understand. Bless their hearts, but they just don't get it, right? But I guarantee there's somebody in your life that just *gets you*, and they're probably right under your nose.

Nobody can understand who A'ja Wilson is without knowing about my grandma, Ms. Hattie Wade Rakes, and everything she stood for.

Grandma was my everything. She was able to see something in me before I even saw it in myself. She had this magic ability to make an introverted, confused, goofy, awkward young girl feel at ease in the world. More than anything, she made me *believe* in myself.

Shoot, I don't think I fully realized what an impact she made on my life until she was gone. I think about what I wouldn't give for just one more afternoon hanging out with her. I may start tearing up just thinking about coming through the front door of her house with my bookbag and getting hit with that cozy smell of coffee roasting on the burner. Mix that with the smell of the furniture in her front room and the newspaper all crinkled up on the table and *The Young and the Restless* blasting on the TV—whoo, Jesus—it's like I'm in a time machine. I can close my eyes, and I'm there with her again.

That was my sanctuary. I could've been having the worst day in the world. I could've flunked my quiz. I could've been dealing with all sorts of middle school drama. I could've gotten my heart broken. Didn't matter. Still doesn't matter, to this very day. My grandma may not be with us anymore, but anywhere I am in the world, I can close my eyes, and I'm there again. I'm warm. I'm safe. I'm *good*.

I feel like every little kid has that one shining light. That one ray of sunshine. Maybe God blesses us with that one angel—*our* person. The person who can fill you up just by the sound of their *voice* when they say your name.

"A'ja, go fix me up a coffee."

"Aww, Grandma!"

"A'ja . . ."

Hit you with the look.

"Alright, Grandma. I'm going. You want milk?"

The older I get, the more I realize you can only connect the puzzle pieces of your life in hindsight. In the moment, you can't see the bigger picture. You can't see how your people are shaping you. And nobody shaped me more than you, Grandma.

How can I make these people understand what a rock you were to us all?

First, you have to know your history. Our history. This was a woman who grew up in the segregated South. She raised four children as a single mother, holding down two jobs. Imagine walking a mile in her shoes during Jim Crow. She lived right by the University of South Carolina, and during segregation, she couldn't even walk through campus to get to the grocery store that was on the other side. She had to walk *around*. And despite all the hatred she lived through, was she bitter? No, no, no. Her whole purpose, no matter who you were, was always: *How can I help?*

You know those people who would give you the shirt off their back? Well, I've literally seen my Ms. Hattie Rakes give somebody the shoes off her feet. And this was when she must have been eighty years old. We were at a funeral for a family friend, and you know how we do it down South. We don't play around. This was not some thirty-minute White People Church. This was some no-nonsense, three-hour Black People Church. I'm talking stockings and skirts, peach pantsuits, men in three-piece suits, everybody and their cousin's cousin dressed-to-the-nines type of atmosphere. This service was naturally going on forever, and we're all standing around in the pews, and you couldn't help but notice this young girl who was really struggling. She was rocking back and forth on her heels. Holding her back. Leaning on the pew. You could tell her shoes were absolutely killing her feet, and the pastor was going on and on. No end in sight. You *know* that struggle. This girl was about to hit the deck.

A couple of minutes later, I look over and see my grandmother standing there rocking a pair of the most *uncomfortable* clogs you've ever seen in your life. I don't even know where these things came from. Like, 1800s Switzerland. I swear they looked like they were wooden, for real. She looked like she was about to go yodeling in the Alps or something.

I'm like, "Grandma, *what?*"

She's like, "Well, the poor girl needed some new shoes. We traded."

I'm like, "You gave her your shoes?"

She's like, "What? These are nice."

I get chills thinking about such a simple memory like that because . . . *phew*. I don't know how to make people really understand, except to say that was my grandmother's main mission in life. To help.

Now, she wasn't a softy!! Let me be clear. She was *hard core* a lot of times. She had to be, with the hand she was dealt. You did not play around with Hattie Rakes. But if she saw somebody who was struggling, it was always, "Are you *good?* You want to trade, honey? I'm alright. You take mine. No, no, no, you take mine."

She was like a *living lesson*. For me. For our family. For our community.

For little A'ja, she was more than a grandmother. She was the foundation, the *roots* of our tree. And how important is that for a young Black girl in America? I used to go to her house literally every single day. The routine was I would go to my grandaddy's house—my daddy's daddy. Then I'd go right down the street to my grandma's house—my mom's mom. It was the perfect combination because my granddaddy was a pastor, and

A'JA WILSON

his house was right next to the church, so there was ab-solutely *no* funny business. Visiting grandaddy was all about *conversation*. No games. No TV. Straight sit-your-butt-down-in-this-chair-and-talk-to-me. We used to be like, "Jesus, Grandaddy, can't we get some cartoons on in here or something? The news? The Weather Chan-nel? *Anything?*"

Nope. Sit with me. Talk with me. About anything or nothing at all. You were lucky to get out of there with some butter cookies. Your main job was to sit there and just absorb his infinite wisdom. It was your little per-sonalized sermon. Right after that, it was straight to my grandma's, and that was a whole different world. Hattie Rakes was about that *action*. She was about those *activi-ties*. Every single day, you knew that TV was cutting off right after *The Young and the Restless*, and that big plastic bag of LEGO blocks was coming out. I can still hear those LEGO blocks jangling around in that big ratchet bag.

"Grandma, nooooo. I don't want to do LEGOs to-day."

"Come on, let's build downtown Columbia!"

"Grandma, do you know how big downtown Co-lumbia is?"

"Come on. Let's start with the colors."

Rule number 1: You absolutely had to start by meticulously sorting the colors of the LEGO blocks, one by one, into perfect little rows. No shortcuts. No complaining. The Hattie Rakes Construction Company did not cut corners. Everything had its place. The project management started from the jump.

"Let's start with the grays."

"Grandma, come ooooonnnn."

"That's going to be our concrete. We'll build the streets first. Oh, honey, I need a coffee."

We'd be sitting on that unforgiving hardwood floor in her front room for hours, just building the streets and the sidewalks and the grass. We're three hours in, and not a single skyscraper has even gone up. Lord, help me! My back is giving out. My knees hurt. I'm like, "Grandma, please. Can we put up a house or something?"

I didn't really understand it at the time, but she was teaching me patience in an impatient world. It's something I think about all the time now because we were genuinely *in the moment*. No phones. No TV. No distractions. It was almost like meditation, in a way. We would sit there for hours and talk while we worked on our miniature Columbia. Time stood still. There was no stress. No problems. No drama. We were in a world of our own.

What a great lesson. When we're kids, we're in such a hurry. As we grow up and become adults, we never learn. In fact, we're in even more of a hurry. We're buried in our phones. Our brains are always stressing about the next thing, the next problem, the next accomplishment. But where are we even *going?* What are we rushing toward? I'm not being funny. Think about it: How much money would you give for just another day with the people you've lost, doing nothing special at all? Just chilling, enjoying each other's company. How much?

I'd give almost anything for just another three hours building LEGO blocks with my grandmother. Every day, just by her being own unique self, she was teaching me how to dream without me even knowing it. She had this map of the world—one of those big plastic maps that everybody used to have in the '90s. I remember she used to spread it out on her dining room table. She had this routine: Whenever somebody in her family traveled anywhere in the world, she would mark the map. As the years went by, it was like watching our family's roots grow all over the world.

"Put a pin where you been, and let's watch it grow."

Subconsciously, without even saying it, she was showing me I could make my mark on the world. That I could leave small-town South Carolina. That I could *be* somebody. I was only six years old, and she'd be saying, "One day soon, I'll be putting dots all over this map for you. Where do you want to go, A'ja?"

I was just a little kid! I was thinking, "Grandma, you're crazy! I don't even have any money! I got five bucks! Where can I go? That'll never be me."

She'd say, "You'll see. You're going to make your mark. Just remember to bring me back some salt-n'-pepper shakers."

OK, so this is probably the most *down South* thing in this entire book. People in California are probably going to be reading this and shaking their heads in confusion. But my grandma used to collect salt-n'-pepper shakers from all over the country and put them on display in her Good Room. She had, like, four shelves of them. Like a shrine. Everywhere you went—no matter if it was down the street or to Alaska—"Bring me back a shaker, honey. Don't forget!" When I finally started traveling for basketball, the number one concern on every trip out of state was where in the heck I was going to find a souvenir shop so I could secure the bag for Grandma.

Of course, it wasn't really *about* the shakers, or the map, or the LEGO blocks. It was always something deeper with my grandma. She was instilling those lessons that only our elders seemed to know how to make stick. Why, twenty years later, do I still vividly remember my grandma putting those dots on that plastic map? Why can I still vividly see her putting a new saltshaker, in the shape of the state of Florida, up on the shelf in her Good Room?

"Grandma, how do you even *get* the salt out of these things? Are these even *usable?*"

It wasn't about the shakers. It wasn't about the map. It was about seeing her roots flourishing. This was a woman who was dealt one of the toughest hands imaginable in life. She sacrificed everything to watch her family grow and thrive. Every new dot on that map was an extension of her—it was her roots spreading across the country, across the world, into places and rooms she hadn't been allowed to reach when she was young.

I wonder. . . . When she was growing up, walking down those streets that were proudly named after prominent slaveholders, walking past those government buildings flying the Confederate flag, walking *around* the college campus that was strictly off-limits to Black Americans, did she imagine that one day her granddaughter would get to attend that same university—on a *scholarship* no less? Could she have ever in a million years dreamed there would be a statue of her granddaughter on those same grounds? That she would travel all the way to Tokyo to represent her country? That she would win a gold medal? That she would be on billboards in New York City?

Did you have that much hope in your heart, Grandma? I know it's selfish of me, but I wish I could ask you now. I wish you were here.

All I know is you were always teaching me to dream bigger than you were allowed to dream. Some of those dreams wouldn't just have been inconceivable, they'd have been illegal. I ask myself all the time if I would have had the strength to walk a mile in your shoes back when you were my age. How were you able to keep your cool when I can barely keep mine now? How were you able to stomach so much in-your-face hatred and still keep your grace and kindness and patience? How were you able to walk all the way around that campus on your way back from the grocery store and still keep a smile on your face for everybody you came across?

Lord, I see *one* mean tweet about myself now, and I want to snap back on 'em and go punch my pillow. I'm only human! How did you do it, Grandma? How could you go through life witnessing so much ugliness and remain such a beacon of light? How were you always the first one to ask, "You *good?* You need some help, honey? You want to trade shoes?"

Even when I went through my Birthday Party drama in the fourth grade, I know how my grandma reacted when my mom told her about it. I can just picture her sitting in her chair, taking the story in calmly, and saying, "Well, you can't be mad at the little girl. She's just repeating what she's seeing and hearing in her house. She's just a child. Don't blame her."

You always saw the good in everybody, Grandma. Even before we could see it in ourselves. For our family, you weren't just the roots. You were the roots, the soil, and the whole dang trunk of our tree. I hope you can see how tall it's still growing, each and every day.

You know, we hear these big words all the time now. On TV commercials. On social media. From companies. Especially when they're marketing to Black women.

"Strong."

"Empowered."

"Resilient."

"Unstoppable."

But words are just words. As Black women, we need to *see* it. Not just on our TV screens, but in real life. Superheroes are one thing . . . real heroes are another.

How many real-life, down-the-block heroes ever get their flowers in our society? Not enough.

I can't even put into words how strong and resilient the Black woman is, because I got to witness the embodiment of it every single day. I got to see somebody walk the walk, not just talk the talk. I got to see somebody who would give you the shoes off her aching feet—at eighty years young, no less, in the middle of a long, hot, endless Southern Baptist sermon.

I got to witness grace personified.

I got to witness you, Grandma.

I wish I could go back and spend another afternoon sorting those gray LEGO blocks with you. No matter how hard we try, we can't stop time. But if our love for somebody is strong enough, maybe we can freeze it. Maybe we can preserve that safe space forever. Maybe we *can* go back, in our hearts. Maybe that's God's gift to us.

Anywhere I am in the world, if I'm having a bad day and life gets to be too overwhelming, I can just close my eyes and take a little trip back to Columbia, South Carolina. I get transported to my grandma's front room, smelling like fresh coffee and old newspaper, and I can hear *The Young and the Restless* theme song on the TV, and that particular sound of my grandma's voice is so soothing. . . .

"*A'ja*, honey."

Thank you, Hattie Wade Rakes. You gave me the ultimate gift. Hope. It was the best gift any young Black woman could ask for. I'm simply glad I got to be your friend.

Your Dreamer,

A'ja Wilson

3

CLICHÉS DON'T STAND A CHANCE AGAINST 13

Dear Black Girls,

This one is for all the girls out there who have ever been called "slow learners."

This is for all the girls who are too scared to put their hand up in class. This is for all the girls who are given a label before they are given a chance.

This is for all the girls who are trying too dang hard, and who are so dang smart, but who just learn a little bit differently.

Girls, I *am* you. When I was sixteen, I was diagnosed with dyslexia. Yes, the woman writing this book you are reading has a learning disability. Let me say it loud, for the folks in the back: Your girl A'ja Wilson has dyslexia, and she's a nationally published author. When I was growing up, this would have seemed like an impossible dream, especially to some of my teachers.

I was always the "slow learner." I was the girl who "didn't understand the instructions." The last one to turn in her quiz. The one who carried around a big stack of flashcards everywhere. The one highlighting everything. The one who never wanted to raise her hand. The one who had to reread that paragraph twice—no, wait, three times. No, wait a second, hold on. . . .

To put it simply, my brain processes language differently than most people. I have a unique way of learning, and that's OK. But for sixteen years of my life, I didn't *know* that. I just thought I wasn't as smart as the other kids.

I was the girl running home to her parents, in tears at the end of the day, crying, "Why does everyone else get it, and I don't? I'm trying, Mom, I *swear*."

Those were some hard days. It felt like I was always a half-step behind. When I read a book, the words on the page were . . . how can I explain this? Jumbled. Mixed up. *Off*. It's like some of the letters were mirrored, flipped, or blurry. Almost like when your laptop starts glitching. Big dense paragraphs that went on forever seemed like a wall of . . . confusion.

So let's break this up, huh?

Phew. That's nice. Let's let this baby breathe.

It wasn't just the letters. I was constantly mixing up

numbers, too. A *9* would become a *6*, in my brain. Or a *6* would . . . wait . . .

Whenever I had to read something in front of my classmates, I'd get really anxious and freeze up, which would make everything worse. The most frustrating part was when I was alone, and I had enough time to get into my comfort zone? To just relax and be free? I was *good*. I loved to write and express myself. The easiest way to convert all the crazy, creative, unexplainable thoughts in my head was to write little stories. I would staple sheets of white computer paper together as my "journal," and I'd write stories about my pet cat that I didn't really have, but in my imagination he definitely existed and was my best friend, and he had superpowers and got up to all sorts of feline adventures around South Carolina.

(See how my brain works?)

I was really fortunate because my parents were able to send me to a private school where I could learn in a smaller classroom. I'm so thankful for their sacrifice, and, trust me, it was a *sacrifice*. They got it from all sides. We lived in a predominantly Black community, and there was always that vibe from certain people of, "Oh, you're sending A'ja over *there*, huh? Well, look at *you*. Y'all must got money, huh? Y'all think you're above us?"

Trust me, my parents would've loved nothing more than to put me in public school. It wasn't about that. I simply couldn't thrive unless I was in the right environment, and thank God they put it all on the line and took *all the smoke* from all sides just to give me that chance.

But it was also complicated because I wasn't just a kid who learned differently, or a girl who learned differently. I was a Black girl who learned differently surrounded by white kids. (And listen! Shout-out to all my white friends and my white teachers! I love you all to death. Miss Ryan, my first-grade teacher, I am still obsessed with you. I still want you to be my BFF. Everything that happened in my first-grade life, it was: "Mom! Mom! I gotta tell Miss Ryan!)

So . . . let me be clear.

Shout. Out. To. My. White. People.

But . . .

Step into my shoes for a second. I already *look* different than everyone else, and now I *think* differently, too? Sheeesh. What am I going to do? I'm just going to retreat into my little shell! My hand is never going up! I'm just an invisible little turtle! Nothing to see here! Don't call on A'ja! *Please*, Jesus!

When you're a little kid, it's not so bad. You're

coasting on coloring books and recess and *Reading Rainbow*. As long as I had a concrete goal or assignment, like memorizing my multiplication tables, I could just work my tail off and conquer it. Our mascot at school was a frog, and so we had this big end-of-the-year test called Ribbit. Oh my God, *Ribbit*. I don't know where the tradition even came from, but every year, whenever you felt like you were ready to rock, you could tell your teacher, "OK, I'm ready for Ribbit."

"You sure, A'ja?"

"I'm ready! I'm ready!"

You got to leave class and walk down to the principal's office for this timed test. But this was more like something you'd see on a reality show. I'm talking rapid-fire questions that you had to answer on your feet with the shot clock running.

"What's twelve times nine?"

Go. Now. Give me an answer! Shot clock's running!

It sounds easy, but not when you only have ten seconds . . . now Nine! Eight! Seven!

Oh my *Gosh*. The anxiety Ribbit caused in my young life, you can't even imagine. I have secondhand anxiety right now just reliving it. They even kept the room cold, like an interrogation room or something. They were trying to throw off your *mental*, I swear.

And by the way, this was not optional. You had to pass Ribbit to move on to the next grade.

If you aced the test, you got a cool frog-themed reward. And they upgraded the swag every rung up the ladder. In second grade, it was a frog bookmark with the crazy frog legs dangling off the page. That was *major* when you got that. Third grade, frog eraser. Extremely dope. In fourth grade, it was a squishy rubber frog that was super cute.

That was the first time in my life I'd learned to lock in. I'm talking about the full-on Kobe *Mamba Mentality*. I had my parents staying up all night doing flash cards with me until I had it down cold. My dad was up in his own head having a crisis, like, "Dang, wait a minute, what *is* 12 times 9? I think I need to redo the fourth grade!"

Looking back on it, those were some amazing bonding times for us as a family. I learned how to channel my anxiety about school into hard work and dedication. But I can't lie to you. When I walked into class the next morning, I was *shaking*. I was more nervous doing Ribbit than playing in the WNBA Finals, for real. It's not even close. I would walk in and immediately tell my teacher, "I can't even start class! Let's go! Ribbit! I'm ready!"

And the thing about Ribbit was there was no hiding.

When you came back into that classroom, everybody knew whether you passed or failed. Either you were hanging your head in shame, or you were holding up that squishy frog in the air like, "Riiiiiiiibbbbbiiiiiiiiiiiit ttttttttttttt!!!!!!!!!!"

Whole class going crazy. "A'ja! A'ja! A'ja! Ribbit! Ribbit!"

I *made it*, y'all!!! I'm *certified*!!!

Those were some good times and definitely some valuable lessons. First through third grade, I was loving my life. But then fourth grade hits. And as we've already established, fourth grade hits *different*.

In fourth grade (why is it always fourth grade???) things got really bad for me. I had a teacher who was . . . let's just be polite and say she was demanding. Let's call her Professor So-and-So. I was terrified of this lady. I don't know why. It just felt like we didn't click. She used to give us these writing exercises, and they would be so vague. She would pass out blank sheets of paper and just write one word on the chalkboard.

BEACH.

"Okay, class. The beach. Take it away!"

I guess it was supposed to inspire creativity? But the only thing it inspired in me was sheer *panic*. My mind started racing a mile a minute. I'm immediately overthinking everything. I'm just staring at this blank white empty void, like, "OK, what can I write about the beach? Maybe I can write about somebody going to the beach for the first time? But then what if everybody thinks I'm writing about myself? What if all these white kids think I've never been to the beach before? What if they think my family is poor? What if they think I can't swim? What if they think . . . ?"

It goes on for five minutes like this, with me trapped inside my own head, and all the while every other kid is just scribbling away like it's *nothing*. Heads down, pencils going crazy, writing freaking *War and Peace* or whatever. They're writing all this about the beach? Am I missing something? We're ten years old!

I'm like, "How in the world???"

I have written *one* sentence down, and little Miss Claire and perfect little William over there are already doing revisions. They got their erasers going crazy, like, "Hmm. No, no, I think I'll remove this paragraph. *Hmm*. Yes. *Indeed*."

I'm like, "The beach? *Really???*"

Finally, by the time I get out of my own head and take a deep breath and start thinking about what I could write that would seem like a story Professor So-and-So would find "proper," she's already walking around the room collecting our papers.

"Pencils down, class! Pencils down!"

It was so embarrassing because I loved to write. But for some reason, I just felt like "I can't possibly let this teacher get inside my head because if she does, she's going to think I'm weird or crazy or—God forbid—*different*."

Oh, Lord. Please, please do not let this terrifying teacher-lady think I'm *different*!

I didn't think the same as William. I didn't think the same as John. I thought how *A'ja* thought.

I didn't know that was perfectly OK.

I felt my teacher wouldn't understand how my brain worked. How is she going to understand that the first thing that came to my mind was a dog who got separated from his family, and he ends up at the beach, and he has to teach himself how to surf so he can get back to his family on the other side of the water, but he also really loves pizza, so he befriends a seagull who shows him how to snatch pepperoni slices from unsuspecting tourists, and . . .

Professor So-and-So wasn't interested in any of that nonsense! She wants perfect paragraphs. She wants

perfect grammar and periods and semicolons and what-
not. She wants "*i* before *e*, except after *c*."

Professor So-and-So doesn't like spelling mistakes,
and the easiest way to not make a mistake? Don't write
anything at all! Just sit there and pray the clock on the
wall goes faster.

This lady wants a normal story from a normal brain,
not the crazy nonsense you're dreaming up, A'ja.

Or at least that's what my anxiety was telling me.
Even back then as a ten year old, I recognized my brain
worked differently. But I saw it as a weakness, not a
strength. So most days, when she would hand us our
writing assignment, I would just stare at the blank white
sheet of paper and go into my shell.

As I got older and started playing basketball, things
only got more complicated because my identity started
to get so mixed up. At school, all my friends were white.
But when I was with my basketball friends on the weekend, everybody on my team was Black. With them, I
was the "Oreo." I was the girl who was "trying to sound
white." (I'm not trying to sound like anything! I'm just
talking! I'm just me!) Just when I started getting comfortable with my basketball friends, the weekend would
be over, and it was back to school again. It was like I

was always trying to keep track of which A'ja I was that day—or which A'ja everyone *expected* me to be.

I couldn't tell my school friends about my crazy basketball stories because they couldn't relate. And I couldn't talk to my basketball friends about my school drama because they would think I was living in *Gossip Girl* or something. It started to feel like I was living a double life.

At least in the fourth grade, when I was freezing up while trying to write about "the beach," I knew who I was. I just couldn't get my thoughts transferred to the page. By the eighth grade, I was so confused that even the dialogue inside my head was complicated.

I remember we had this writing class with a teacher named—I kid you not—Mr. Gatsby. He was like a character out of a movie. He had been at my school for, like, fifty years, and he was legendary. He had the old-school Southern voice. He would be rocking the seersucker suit every day. He even wore a bowtie. He was everything you picture a Mr. Gatsby to be. You never wanted to disappoint Mr. Gatsby. But the setup of the class was so creepy because it was just a bunch of desks with laptops that faced the walls. I guess it was supposed to help us lock in and forget about the world and concentrate on our writing, but to me, it just felt so stressful.

Mr. Gatsby would give us an assignment, and we'd face the wall, looking at a blank Microsoft Word document, and he'd be pacing back and forth behind us. *Looming. Lurking.* Or at least that was what I thought. All you could hear was the click-clack of the keyboards all around you. It was scary, y'all! Every time I tried to type out a sentence, I could imagine him going "*Hmm. Nope.*"

Delete, delete, delete.

But that's not even the cherry on top. The cherry is you would turn in your poems or your haikus or whatever by email, and then Mr. Gatsby would project them on the screen in front of the whole class and give you *feedback.* In front of everybody! On poetry! Your innermost thoughts! Exposed to the world! Up on that big TV!

Can you imagine something more terrifying??? I mean, come on! Is there no justice in this cruel world? Why you gotta do us like this, Mr. Gatsby???

You already know what happened next. I froze up. Whenever he would give us an assignment, I would just sit there staring at that blinking cursor, trying to figure out what people wanted me to write. Not what *I* wanted to write. Not what was actually going on inside my head. Not my real thoughts. That was way too scary.

I was obsessed with trying to fit in when I should have embraced standing out. I would look at that blinking cursor, wondering how to write the *perfect* thing. But what was in my head wasn't perfect. It was confusing, weird, funny, complicated, interesting, boring, Black, white, city, bougie, country, strange, here-and-there-and-everywhere.

Not perfect. Not what they wanted.

So, in the end, I wouldn't write anything until the last five minutes of class. Or I would write four lines and then delete them all. I would wait until the bell rang to send in my assignment and then dip out of there as quick as I could. Anything to save myself from the embarrassment of sharing my words with the class.

Every time I attempted to express myself—to put a little bit of me on the page—I got scared. Part of it was I was still trying to figure out who A'ja actually *was*. What was my identity? What was my core? When I was with my grandmother or my parents, I felt I had a good idea who A'ja was. But when I was with my friends? It was kind of like my dyslexia. Everything was . . . jumbled. Blurry. Mixed up. Confusing.

I wish I could go back and tell myself, "You don't have

to pick a side. Don't worry about being the Black Girl or the White Girl. Don't worry about what these teachers think of you. Don't worry about being different. Just be *you*." But that's easy to say now, at twenty-seven years old. At eleven? Twelve? *Thirteen?* (*Oh, Lord*, thirteen.)

Girls, you know how hard it is. There's no cliché in the world—no advice, no book, no magic wand—that can make thirteen easy. For girls. For boys. Black, white, Asian, everyone.

"Just be you" doesn't stand a chance against *thirteen*.

Listen, I was just as lost as you've been.

I can't tell you how to act. How to think. How to express yourself. I don't have a cheat code.

All I can do is tell you my story.

I've never told anybody this before, but when I was in the first grade—when I was still just innocent little A'ja in her barrettes, without a care in the world, my mom asked me what I wanted to be when I grew up.

Guess what I said?

The audacity of this little girl!

The dyslexic one. The "slow learner." The one who always needed extra time. The girl who never raised her hand. The girl who handed in a blank page. The girl who always went into her shell. The girl who was terrified to express herself.

Yes, that girl.

That girl said, "I want to tell stories. I want to be an author."

Heyyyyyy, look at your girl now. We can tell our stories how we want. There's no one right way. There's an exception to every rule.

So, to all my "slow learners" out there . . .

Remember: Life is a marathon, not a sprint. Embrace your pace. Embrace your *different*. Dream your dreams. And don't let those haters tell you *nothing*.

Passionately,

Aja Wil~

4

QUEEN OF MEDIOCRE

Dear Black Girls,

This one is for all the girls out there who are sitting at the end of the bench.

This is for all the girls out there who can't walk and chew gum at the same time.

This is for all the girls out there who are uncomfortable in their own skin.

This is for all the girls who have no clue what "their thing" is.

This is for all my late, late, *late* bloomers.

I was just like you. I swear to you. I was not a natural. I was not born with a jump shot and basketball in my crib. I know that sounds weird for somebody who ended up going number one in the WNBA Draft, but you can ask anyone I grew up with in South Carolina.

A'ja Wilson was the queen of mediocre. It wasn't for a lack of trying. Oh, I tried *everything*. I was many things before I was a basketball player. A soccer player, a volleyball player, a dancer, a ballerina. I tried 'em all, and I was a solid 4-out-of-10 at 'em all.

It was like, "Man, what's my *thing?*" Tried piano. Fell asleep on the keys. Tried tap dancing. Tapped out. Ballet was poppin' for a minute, but then we had our first real recital, and they had the place so dark that I freaked out and wouldn't come out from behind the curtain. I was like, "Where's my parents? I'm not coming out on that stage until I can see my parents. Y'all see my mom out there? Why can't we just turn the lights on, people?"

The instructor got me out onstage somehow, and when the music started playing, every one of my friends were out there *Black Swan*-nin' around the stage, being perfect little ballerinas, and I was standing still in the middle of the stage, completely frozen. Stiff as a board. Not moving at all. I'm just looking out into the audience, like, "Mom? Where's my mom? Too dark in here. I hate this. Maybe if I don't move, people won't see me."

I finally just walked right off the stage in the middle of the performance. I'm Out. Goodbye. Exit, Stage Left. My mom said she came running, looking for me, thinking I was going to be crying my eyes out. But she found me in the snack line in the reception area, eating some chips. Crunchin' away like nothing happened. She said, "A'ja you can't just *do that!*"

I said, "Why not? I wasn't feeling it!"

That was the end of my ballet career.

The literal last thing on my mind was basketball. Basketball? All that sweating? All those guys on TV mean-mugging each other and talking trash and looking so serious? No, no, no. That's not for me. I'm a princess. That's way too much for me. I'm just trying to chill.

But my dad is a basketball *nut* (more on him in a minute), but he knew if he ever tried to pressure me into playing ball, it was going to be a long day for him.

One day, when I was ten years old, I finally dipped my toe into basketball. I signed up for a coed rec league, and I was the only girl on my team. You already know how this story goes. All those boys did not want to pass me the ball. I'd be wide open, flailing my arms, and they wouldn't even look my way. To be fair to them, I was so skinny that my socks wouldn't even stay up, and it was an accomplishment for me to run down the court without looking like a baby giraffe on ice.

Of course, since I'm not getting the ball, my mind starts wandering. I'm just kind of walking around as the ball is going back and forth. Then, out of the blue, I don't know what happened, but I see that orange leather bouncing toward me.

I grab the basketball. I feel the leather. I look up. It's like a movie. There's no one in front of me. I see the hoop at the other end of the court. And I just take off. No more baby giraffe now. I'm like a cheetah. Everything is a blur. I'm leaving all the boys in the dust. And I can literally hear the whole gym going crazy like, "A'ja! A'ja!" I'm thinking: Let's gooooooo, girl. This is it. This is your calling.

I fly into the lane, uncontested. And right as I'm about to jump up for an easy layup, I hear one of the boys on my team screaming, "A'ja! You're going the wrong way! A'ja, noooooooooooooo!"

I am not leaving anybody in the dust. I am not a cheetah. I am simply going the wrong way. I am shooting on the wrong hoop. I am the single most embarrassed person in the state of South Carolina, maybe in the whole world, the whole dang universe. Nothing could be worse than this moment. I am in mid-air, and I am about to score on our own hoop. And then somehow, it gets worse.

I brick the layup. Clank. I couldn't even score on our own hoop.

I grab my own rebound. I'm just staring at everybody, wide eyed. The whole gym is quiet. The boys got their hands up like, *What in the world?*

I look over at my parents on the sideline. They got their hands up like, *A'ja. A'ja. Child. Are you serious?*

And then I just sit down right under the hoop, and I start bawling.

"I wanna go home. I hate basketball. I hate these boys. This is stupid. I wanna go home."

I had a meltdown in front of everybody. I would not get up. I don't know what I expected to happen, but the boys didn't even flinch. They grabbed the ball and just kept playing around me while I sat there in a puddle of my own tears. My mom is sitting on the bleachers looking at me like, *A'ja, if you think I'm coming out there to get you, then you must be crazy. Stand up on your own two feet.*

I sat there for about two minutes before I got up. I told myself, "I am never going to pick up a basketball again. This is the dumbest sport in the world."

It was so bad and so embarrassing that to this very day, whenever we're coming out of a TV timeout in the WNBA, I go up to one of the refs and I ask, "Alright, which way is Vegas going? That way? Cool, just double-checking."

For years after my meltdown, I wanted nothing to

do with basketball. I associated it with only two things: mean people and sweat. But then when I got to the eighth grade, right around the time I really started to struggle in school with my undiagnosed dyslexia, identity, and self-confidence, life decided to throw me another nice little curveball. God blessed me with a ridiculous growth spurt. I guess it wasn't enough for A'ja Wilson to be the asthmatic, dyslexic, left-handed, failed-pianist, uncoordinated, skinny Black girl. No, that was too basic.

Let's add another twist. Hit her with the growth spurt. Now she's got to be a head taller than the boys. Thank you, Lord. The boys are gonna love that.

Seventh grade A'ja was a hot mess of emotions. Oh yes, puberty hits *different*. Imagine being me. I think different than everybody. I look different than everybody. I don't have a special talent. If you had asked me what my passion in life was at age thirteen, I'd have probably said "I like to make goofy videos with my friends in iMovie?" (I guess I was an influencer before influencing, but that wasn't getting me anywhere in 2009.)

I was lost.

I just kind of shrugged my shoulders and said to basketball, "Alright, I'm tall. Why not?" In the movie version of my life, we would skip ahead here: I would go to the gym with my dad, and he would put the ball in my hands with *Rocky* music playing in the background. And I would just start conquering the world. But that is not, in fact, what happened at all.

What happened was I was extremely bad at the game of basketball. Awful. Trash. Go ahead and ask my own father. He'll tell you. He was my first coach when I started playing "for real" at thirteen.

My whole childhood, he was so resistant to pushing me into basketball because it was too close to home for him. He never made it to the NBA, but he played professionally in Europe for years. Did you ever wonder how I got my name? That was all my dad. He gave me that name twenty years before I was even born. See, my dad was the original Most Interesting Man in the World. In the late '70s, he was chilling with his teammates in the South of France, and the band Steely Dan was playing this song called "Aja." (Pull it up on Spotify, and you'll get the vibes.) The way he tells it, he was drinking some wine and eating some cheese, and he turned to his teammates and said, "You know what? If I ever have a little girl, I'm going to name her A'ja."

They were all probably looking at him like, *Alright, buddy, you lit. You need to hydrate.*

So this is the character we are dealing with, just to

paint the picture. He waited twenty years for his daughter, and he never forgot that night on the French Riviera.

From day one, he was always riding with me no matter what I wanted to do. He waited until I told him I wanted to try basketball, and even then it was like, "You sure? Because if you're in, I'm all in. But you gotta be sure."

I started playing in some church leagues, and I was doing OK. When I was thirteen, my dad and a friend actually started this travel team because they didn't like the politics of AAU (that's the fancy travel basketball league, for my non-hoops fans). They didn't like how certain girls always got to play because their dad was the coach or whatever. They were going to do it a different way. They were going to do it right. And that was exactly my problem. I was the coach's daughter, so you would think I'd be getting automatic minutes no matter how bad I was, but whenever we'd come home from a travel tournament, I wouldn't even have to put my jersey in the dirty laundry. It was fresh as a daisy. I'd be sitting there clapping for two hours straight. I never moved from that bench.

One day, I asked my dad why I never got in the game and he said, "Do you want me to be honest?"

"Be honest."

"*Honest* honest?"

"Yes."

"A'ja do you think I like doing this? Spending three grand a summer to drive to all these tournaments? Do you think I like to see my daughter on the bench? I hate it. I'm never going to push you to do something you don't want to do, but I'm also never going to lie to you. So do you really want me to be honest with you?"

"Yes, Daddy."

"A'ja, honey . . . what can I say? You're trash."

Now, we have a pause. We need to talk about my father for a minute. I don't want y'all to get the wrong impression. I *love* my father. My father is my best friend in a lot of ways. But, girls, you know how it is. We all got that one person in our life who . . . how can I put this?

That person who . . .

Arrrrrghhhhhh!!!!

It's impossible to capture it all in a single word.

Your road dog. Your coach. Your nemesis. Your mentor. The person who never sugarcoats it. The person you either want to call immediately whenever something happens, or the person who makes you put your phone on Do Not Disturb. The one who always keeps it real—and sometimes a little *too real*.

For me, that's my dad.

57

Sometimes, it can be hard to appreciate those people, especially when you're going through an awkward time in your life. Especially when you're thirteen, fourteen, fifteen—they're the last voice you want to hear because they tell you the truth. And when you're thirteen, fourteen, fifteen? Girl, the truth *hurts*.

But ask yourself this question: How does a late bloomer finally bloom? They need a gardener in order to grow, right? Well, think of this person as your gardener.

If you don't know who your gardener is, ask yourself, "Who is that person who always has my back, even when we don't see eye to eye?"

My dad was my gardener, and the greatest thing about him was he was always *there*.

Rain or shine, he was always going to show up for me. Anything I was into, he was into. When I was into volleyball, he came home from work with an inflatable beach ball so we could practice in the living room. When I was into ballet, he'd pretend he was prancing around with me. When I just wanted to play The Floor Is Lava, he'd jump around from couch to couch with me. We turned everything into a game. We turned life itself into nothing but fun.

When I got older and hit my growth spurt and hated

my legs, hated wearing dresses, hated everything about being in my own skin? He'd always tell me, "A'ja, you are so beautiful. You don't even know how beautiful you are. I'm so proud of you."

And of course, I'd be rolling my eyes and saying, "Uggggh. Dad, you don't get it. Leave me alone!!!!"

Without my father, I wouldn't be who I am today. But that doesn't mean our relationship was easy. He told me what I needed to hear, not what I wanted to hear. That's a dynamic I don't see represented enough in movies and books. It's always so black and white. We usually see someone who is either your biggest fan or your biggest critic. But sometimes, your biggest fan *is* your biggest critic. I think it's hard for girls to deal with this kind of relationship when they're teenagers, especially Black girls.

As Black women, we are so hard on ourselves. That voice inside our own heads is so harsh and so negative. The easiest way to get a break from that voice is to seek out people who are going to tell us what we want to hear, who are going to tell us we're the greatest thing since sliced bread. Even when we know it's insincere and toxic, it feels so good to hear that sometimes, right?

It's one of those lessons that doesn't sink in until you really go through some things in life: If everybody around you is telling you what you want to hear? Girl, you made a wrong turn. You got off at the wrong exit. You better turn around and go find your people.

The irony of my relationship with my dad was that the better I got at hooping, the more complicated it became for us. After I hit my growth spurt, I started asking him to push me harder and harder. I'd stay after our practices and strap on a forty-pound weight vest, and he would run me through extra conditioning. Basketball gave me a confidence I didn't have before. When I put on my basketball uniform and gripped that orange leather and was with my teammates, everything just made sense. I had an identity. I had a passion. I had my *thing*.

And by the way, girls, your thing definitely does not have to be sports. It could be piano or computer programming or painting or anything under the sun. But when you get into your *zone* and everything is just flowing for you, and you're happy and confident and you can't wait to wake up the next morning and do that thing again? That's it. Your thing. You shouldn't second-guess it or worry about what other people think. If the vibes are good, and it's giving you confidence, then you should just dive into it with everything you got.

When I was sixteen, I got the invitation to go try out for the USA Basketball Junior National Team in Colorado Springs. I literally thought I was traveling there just to be one of the easy cuts. "Hello, thanks for the invite; thanks for the T-shirt" kind of a thing. I was the youngest girl there. Most of the other girls were eighteen years old. They were super-duper stars in my eyes. Breanna Stewart. Kelsey Plum.

I remember my dad being like, "A'ja, they're not inviting you out there for no reason. You got a chance."

"Alright, coach. Whatever."

I'm sixteen. I know everything, right? I'll never forget—after three days of camp, they kicked all the families and everyone out of the gym, and they locked the doors. It was just us and the coaches, and they were announcing who made the team.

Somehow, I had made the cut. In the span of six years, I went from crying on the floor of the gym to representing my country. It was really overwhelming.

You'd think this is the happy ending. Everything from here on out would be gravy.

Team USA.

South Carolina.

The W.

Trophies.

TV commercials.

Shoe deals.

But life is not a movie.

Within a few weeks, I was literally threatening to quit basketball. My life had never been so good, and I had never felt so anxious and so afraid.

Everyone always talks about the fear of failure. But the thing I never hear anyone talk about is the fear of success.

You hear about "impostor syndrome" all the time, but I don't think that totally captures it. I knew I wasn't an impostor. I knew I was finally good at something. But the minute it felt like basketball could change my life?

No.

I don't want my life to change! I like my life. I like my friends. I like my routine and my inside jokes and my comfort zone!

Shoot, I *finally* got comfortable, and now you're telling me basketball could take me into a whole new world with a new set of pressures and a new set of people I don't know?

PASS. I'm good.

After I made the Junior National Team, everything became too *real*. My emotions were all over the place.

I'd be in the gym with my dad and having a rough day, so he'd be yelling at me to pick up the pace—not as my father, but as my coach.

And one time, I just snapped. I remember one day I was missing free throws, and he was yelling at me to concentrate. I threw the ball back at him and asked, "Do you love me?"

He was shocked. He was in coach mode, and he was like, "What?"

I said, "No, seriously. Do you actually love me?"

"Of course I love you. What are you talking about?"

"If you loved me, you wouldn't be talking to me like this." I told him, "Just put me up for adoption. I don't want you to be my coach. I want you to be my *dad*."

For a few weeks, I really struggled. I told my mom I didn't want my dad to come to the gym with me anymore. I told her I wanted to quit basketball and go back to my normal life.

I had the whole world in front of me, and all I wanted to do was lay in my bed underneath my covers.

I was scared of change.

I was scared of success.

Thankfully, I had that person in my life who was never afraid to be a little too real with me. I had my gardener: my dad.

He sat me down one night, and he didn't preach to me. He didn't give me some big speech. He looked me dead in my eyes and said, "A'ja, if you want me to be your coach, I'll be your coach. If not, that's cool. If you want to stop playing basketball, that's cool, too. But I'm talking to you as your dad right now. I feel like you're pretty dang good at this basketball thing. I feel like it could take you so many places in this world. If *you* want it, then I want it. If *you* want it, I'll do whatever it takes to help you. Whatever you decide, I'll love you any-way."

The point of this story is not that I stuck with basket-ball. The point is not that I got to go all around the world with the Junior National Team. The point is not that I got a scholarship or made it to the WNBA. The point is not about basketball.

The point is that my dad gave me a choice. He kept it real with me without ever pressuring me. He allowed me to be scared. He allowed me to be *sixteen*. For a young Black girl who was so unsure of herself for so long, it's one of the best gifts I could've ever asked for. My dad wasn't always perfect. But he was always *there*.

One of the things I didn't understand in the moment was how fine of a line he was walking all the time. You have to remember: my father is a six-foot-eight Black man in the South. He's got the big booming voice and the muscles (at least back then! Sorry, Pops!) He's got this *presence* about him. He even used to rock one of those big '70s trench coats like he was Marvin Gaye. Every time my father walked into a gym, all eyes were on him. He loved me so much, and he was so passionate about basketball, that his energy radiated. It could be too much for people. Shoot, it could even be too much for my mom! He would be so stressed out at my games that she didn't even want to sit next to him half the time.

If we were in a certain part of town, playing against the all-white teams, that could be a real problem. You could see the looks the parents on the other team would be giving each other.

If that same energy was coming from a five-foot-eight white dentist wearing a Patagonia vest? It would've been a much different vibe.

They'd be saying, "Oh, that's just Jason. He's so passionate about his girls. #GirlDad!"

People were intimidated by my dad because of the way he looked. They saw him as a threat. There were a few times when somebody in the gym even called security on my dad. I'd be out on the floor in the middle of a game, and I'd see the security guards talking to my dad, and him trying to be calm about everything and explain there was no problem—that he was just trying to cheer for his daughter.

Imagine being in his shoes. There were so many times when he could have just walked away. He could have stopped showing up to my games. Or worse, he could have stopped being himself. He could have sat way up in the bleachers and bit his knuckles all game, not saying a word. But that was never our relationship. That was not who I wanted him to be. I wanted him to push me and motivate me. Basketball wasn't just my thing. It was *our* thing. Whether it was The Floor Is Lava or ballet or hide-and-go-seek, everything was *our thing*.

My dad isn't perfect. But I wouldn't trade my dad for any other dad in the world. Because he never stopped showing up for me.

For all my late bloomers out there, I know how awkward and confusing and frustrating life can feel. I know how lonely it can seem, too. But I guarantee you that somewhere out there, you have your own gardener.

Ask yourself: Who's that person who is always trying to bring out the best in you? The person who drives you crazy, makes you laugh, challenges you, pushes you to be a better person, and has the courage to show you *both* kinds of love—the easy kind and the tough kind?

That's your gardener. Remember to always keep them close.

Without our gardeners, we would never grow. We would never flourish. We would never bloom.

Your girl,

Aja Wil

5

THE NONSENSE DETECTOR

Dear Black Girls,

This one is for the girls having a major glow-up.

This is for all the girls who are killing the game right now.

This is for all the girls who are feeling themselves a *liiiittle bit* too much right now.

Oh yes, I said it. You know who you are.

You're starting to get a little attention, and you're liking it a little bit too much.

Don't try to act like you don't know what I'm talking about.

All your awkward days are over, huh? It's a New You. You got your Beyoncé going in the headphones. Maybe the college letters are coming in. Couple people in your DMs. Maybe your LinkedIn is popping. First job offers rolling in. Yes, I see you.

You got your whole life ahead of you, and everybody is telling you whatever you want to hear all of a sudden.

I mean, how can you *not* be feeling yourself? It's OK. I know how it is. I've *been* there.

All I'm saying is: careful.

Watch yourself! That's all I'm saying.

Listen, I know how it feels when you go from being a nobody to a sorta-somebody. It happened to me almost overnight.

I remember when I got my first college recruiting letter in the mail; I barely even knew what it meant to be recruited. We got this envelope from UNC–Greensboro. And when I read the letter, talking about how they wanted me to come to their school, I ran in to the other room and told my mom, "Oh, my God! These people want to pay for my degree? Were they watching the right A'ja Wilson? They were watching number 22, right? Is this for real? I'M SO GOING TO UNC–GREENSBORO! . . . WHERE'S GREENSBORO?"

My mom was just looking at me like, *Mmmm-hmmm. OK, child. Relax.*

I could have never navigated through that moment in my life without my mom. My mom was like the security guard outside the park, making sure nobody was going to come in and trample all over the flowers. Eva Wilson does not play around. She is about her business. Especially when it comes to her family. If you try some slick talk around Eva Wilson, she will absolutely dismantle you.

"Sorry, can you repeat that? What was that you said? I want to dig a little deeper on that, sir, because in my notes here . . ."

So, naturally, she was the perfect person to be by my side when I started getting some attention from the world.

Now, here's the tricky thing. As Black women, we are so used to being ignored, talked down to, cast aside, devalued. When you grow up being so used to that bias, it's only natural to fall into the trap of craving that kind of attention. It's like: Excuse me! Over here! Hand us the microphone. Give us our due. Let us have our moment in the sun.

But then when it actually *happens?* And all of a sudden, you have friendly smiling people telling you everything you want to hear, promising you things, wanting a little piece of you?

Careful. If it feels too good to be true, then you already *know* what it is.

As Black women, we have a superpower inside of us.

To keep it PG-13, let's call it your Nonsense Detector. And when that detector is flashing red when somebody is trying to sell you a dream, you need to trust it.

The problem is, we are only human, right? When you're so used to being ignored and all of a sudden fancy people are coming to you telling you that you're "ah-mazing," it can be intoxicating.

Your head can start spinning.

You can start second-guessing your detector, thinking you're just being paranoid. Hey, maybe these people are right. Maybe I am ah-mazing. Maybe I should just trust whatever they're saying. Maybe I was just being crazy. Maybe the world really is my oyster. Who needs to read the fine print anyway? That itty-bitty print way down there? Who got time for that? These fancy people definitely have my best interests at heart.

Right?

Right?

Pssshhh. Girl. You better have somebody in your life you can count on to push back and say, "Hang on. Excuse me a moment, sir. One question on that . . ."

Because everything happened so fast for me with basketball, my head was spinning from the sudden attention. I remember the mailman coming to our house every day after school, and, at first, he'd have, like, one recruiting letter a week mixed in with the magazines and the bills, and it was so exciting. We would stick the letters up on the refrigerator like trophies. Then I started getting more attention, and the mailman would walk up to our front door with three or four letters and a big smile on his face, and I remember him saying, "Don't worry, I'll have more for you tomorrow." I'll never forget getting my first letter from a big school, because it came in this orange envelope. I saw that tiger paw on the front, and that's when I was like, "Wow, Clemson? ACC Basketball? A'ja Wilson in the ACC? Dang." By the time I was a junior, we had so many letters that we had to go out and buy one of those huge plastic storage crates from Bed Bath & Beyond. When we filled that one up and had to go buy another, that was when my mom started telling me, "A'ja, you know your life is about to change, right? You need to be prepared for it. We need to take this seriously."

For an introvert like me, it was a lot to take in. My mom could tell it was going to my head. We got a letter from the University of Hawaii one day, and I was trying to convince my mom to let me go on a visit. She hit me with the stern, "Hawaii, A'ja? Really?"

I did my best to fake it. "What? I'm really interested."

"We're not flying ten hours on a plane to no Hawaii

so you can sit on the beach sipping on some coconuts. Get serious, child. This isn't a vacation. This is your life."

"But, Mom! But . . ."

"A'ja, last week, you called me in hysterics because you had to fill out a form at the post office. You're going to go to college in *Hawaii?* Halfway around the world when you can't go halfway around the block. Really?"

Shut down. End of conversation. She would be hitting me with the reality checks that only moms can provide. Sometimes, she would just look at me and say "*A'ja.*" That look contained a whole bunch of examples of why I was acting crazy, but she couldn't even be bothered to verbalize them.

Just . . . "*A'ja.*"

But she was completely right. I was still so naive and unprepared for the world. All it took was some school to show some interest in me, to *want me,* and I was like a little puppy dog. When I got invited to the Elite Camp at the University of South Carolina, it was so surreal, because I had actually been at one of their summer camps when I was around twelve years old, but under totally different circumstances. I called it a "Day Care Camp." They used to put on these (alleged!) basketball camps for kids in the local area every summer, and it was like an easy way for parents to stuff their kids in a gym during summer vacation so they didn't have to pay twenty bucks a day for a babysitter. South Carolina tried to make it this super official, cool thing with all this free Gamecocks swag and this tour of their facilities and everything, like we were some real recruits, but I saw right through it. I'm like, "Y'all really got us in here playing the egg race with the kitchen spoon, and you think I'm falling for this? We're out here playing It-Tag. These kids can't even dribble! I know why my mom sent me here! I know I'm trash at basketball! This is day care!"

God bless them; they even had this certificate ceremony for us at the end of the camp, and they had Dawn Staley come out and present us with this piece of paper with a gold star on it. That was the first time in my life I ever met Coach Staley. The camp counselor called me up to the stage, Coach handed me this embarrassing piece of paper, and we smiled for a picture. And in my head I'm like, "Alright. Thanks. I got my Certificate of Good Behavior and my GAMECOCKS T-shirt. I get it. I'm *that kid*."

In the span of two years, I went from the Day Care Camp to the Elite Camp. As I kept climbing up the national rankings, Dawn would show up to my AAU games to watch me. She'd be sitting there wrapped up in her zebra blanket, too cool for school, not really even saying anything. Just watching me, honoring me with her presence. (Sorry, Dawn.)

You would think that with South Carolina being in my backyard, and Dawn being Dawn, I would've been over the moon. But if you think that, then you don't remember being sixteen! I was feeling myself! I was such a little punk. I was telling my mom, "I'm not staying in South Carolina. I need to spread my wings."

I thought I was so smart. Nobody could tell me *nothing.* And when I made that first recruiting visit to Chapel Hill? It was over.

The minute I stepped onto that campus and saw the facilities and the vibes and—alright I'll be honest with you; it wasn't about any of that. What really happened was I saw the boys.

To be fair to me, UNC absolutely set me up. They had the slickest recruiting trick I have ever seen. They actually took me over to this diner called Time-Out. It's kind of an iconic spot on campus where all the students go to hang out at night. So we get there and sit down in the booth, and this really cute guy comes over to take my order, like, "You want something to drink?"

Cool, cool. We order. Already my mom is looking at me extremely skeptical, like: *Hmm. My radar is going off.*

The next thing we know, a couple players from the UNC men's basketball team come and bring me my iced tea.

Super polite, big smiles. Asking my mom, "Ma'am, anything else we can get you?"

I'm looking at my mom all doe-eyed, like, "Are you seeing this? Is this real? Um. It's over. I love it here. Call up the coaches. Call up the dean. Sign the papers. I'm coming to UNC. It's a wrap."

I don't think we had even spoken to a single person yet. We were on one of those walking tours, looking at some random building, and I was already ready to sign away my future because I saw a couple cute boys walking around. Thankfully, my mom held it down for me.

"A'ja. *A'ja.* You cannot be this naive. THIS IS A SETUP, CHILD. THIS IS NOT REAL LIFE."

I was huffing the whole way home, like, "Mom, just let me live!"

Needless to say, she made us look at more schools. To say she was meticulous about my college process would be the understatement of the century. She created her own Excel spreadsheet to evaluate every aspect of the schools. She would come on the visits carrying around this iPad, and she would be grilling everybody—the coaches, the administrators, random students. She didn't even care if you were a head coach. She was trying to vibe-check you at all times, to make sure her daughter was going to be in good hands. I think she even had a section labeled BODY LANGUAGE.

My dad's first question was always, "How many hours can she be in the gym a week?"

And my mom would say, "No, no, no. Disregard my husband. Strike that from the record, please. We're talking education right now. How many hours can she meet with the tutor per week?"

They were the perfect balance. I remember one coach was really selling us on a dream, and it just felt like a little too *extra*, you know? They're giving off a little bit of that used-car salesman vibes, and my mom just cuts them off and says, "Excuse me. This all sounds so rosy. But, just to be clear, my daughter is going to college with or without basketball. She doesn't *need* this to get her degree. So we don't need to hear things that are too good to be true."

Whenever I was getting a little too excited about the glitz and glamor of a school—anything that didn't have to do with academics or basketball—she'd say, "Oh, that razz your jazz, huh? OK. Interesting."

And she'd make a little *tick* on her spreadsheet.

It was like, "OK, we're going to follow up on that later. We need to talk about that in more detail."

As a Black woman who had seen so much more of the world than I had, she knew she had to protect me from myself.

Without my mom, I would've been chewed up and spit out by the world the minute it started showing me some love. She made me take a hard look at people's words, what was behind those words, and—most important of all—she challenged me to think about their intentions.

Is this person coming from a genuine place?

Is what they're saying a little too perfect?

Are they selling me a dream?

Is my Nonsense Detector going off, and I just don't want to listen to it?

As a young Black woman, nonsense detection is one of the most important skills you can learn. How you process success is going to be just as important as how you process failure. When everything is popping for you, can you maintain your perspective? Can you guard your soul? Do you have the right people around you?

My mom was always reminding me to see what was behind people's words. She valued intention over everything.

I knew that, deep down, she wanted me to stay close to home.

She wanted me to build my own legacy in South Carolina.

She wanted me to play for Dawn Staley, a strong Black woman who was not going to be afraid (I repeat: NOT GOING TO BE AFRAID) of pulling me into her office and telling me straight to my face, "Girl, you are messing up right now."

My mom knew Coach Staley would never be calling me out.

She was going to be calling me *in*. As in *into her office* for a reality check when I was feeling myself a little too much.

But at the end of the day, the beautiful thing about both my mom and dad was they never pressured me to do anything. They left the decision up to me. And, boy, did I have fun with that power. Once I whittled my decision down to the last four schools, I purposely didn't tell anyone in my family what I was going to do. I was running so much misdirection, keeping everybody on pins and needles.

Well, everybody except one person.

When I was preparing to make my decision, weighing all my options, one thing that broke my heart was going somewhere far away, like Connecticut or even Tennessee, and not being able to pop in and visit my grandma.

She never said anything to me about it. She never gave me any guilt trip about leaving her. She always wanted to see me spread my wings and fly. But one day I was over at her house, like usual, and she was watching *The Young and the Restless* and drinking coffee, and I told her, "You know I'm going to keep visiting you when I go to college, right, Grandma?"

She said, "Oh, I know. I'm not worried about it."

I said, "I won't be far away. I'm going to be right down the road, so I can come visit you whenever I want. You know I can't leave you."

She never made a big deal out of it because that was just her way, but I know how proud it made her. When she was my age, she couldn't even walk through the University of South Carolina campus as a Black woman. Now her granddaughter was going there on a full scholarship to play basketball under a Black female head coach.

I said, "You know what that means though, right? My first game, you have to come see me play."

She promised me she would come. "Well, I don't care about the game. But I'll come and keep my eyes on you. Make sure those girls don't be pushing on you too much."

I waited until the very last minute to tell my family where I was going to school. My mom was bursting at the seams. I guess I got way too good at playing it cool, because when I called Dawn Staley on the phone to tell her my decision, my whole family said I was so somber and serious that they thought I was telling her I was going somewhere else. Even Dawn tells me to this day, "You sounded like you were at a funeral. I thought you were going to UConn":

Um, hey, Coach. Yeah, I just wanted to tell you that um . . . thank you for everything and . . . I'm coming to South Carolina.

When I tell you my whole family went crazy . . . they went crazy-crazy-crazy. For us, that moment was about so much more than basketball. Listen, South Carolina has its problems. No place is perfect.

But at the end of the day, the people of South Carolina cared about A'ja Wilson before anybody even knew me as "A'ja Wilson." When I was just a little kid running offstage at my ballet recital and shooting on the wrong basketball hoop, when I was just a little kid with asthma and dyslexia who could not walk and chew gum at the same time, and when I was the only person who looked like me in a room. . . .

Honestly? Most of the people in my community had my back. I had so many great teachers and friends and mentors who just *got me*, whether they looked like me or not. South Carolina is more than my home. South Carolina *is* me.

Why do you think they call them your roots, anyway?

They keep you grounded. They keep you *solid*.

I didn't want to be just one of a million banners up in the rafters at UConn. I wanted to create history in my own backyard. I wanted my grandma to walk proudly across those campus grounds, and sit in the front row, and watch her granddaughter play for the first time.

I wanted her to see that she was right about me with her own eyes. My first year at South Carolina, our first home game was against Coker University, and Grandma was sitting courtside. VIP. With her own special chair and everything. They made sure she was right on the corner of our bench, at her request. She had no interest in watching the game. Her eyesight was so bad by that point it was probably all a blur, anyway. But all she wanted to do was watch her granddaughter. "Point me toward A'ja, and I'm good."

She kept her promise.

Less than a year later, she was gone. On one of her last good days on earth, she got to see me shine. I thank God we got to share that moment together. I thank God I didn't go chasing banners at UConn, or chasing boys at North Carolina, or chasing some idea of "The New A'ja" halfway across the country.

I chose to stay at home, close to the people I love, and write my own story.

Black girls, I can't tell you how to make the big decisions in your life. When I was going through it, I was just as confused as you might be now.

The only advice I can give you is this . . .

We're always in such a hurry to spread our wings. If it's right for you to leave the nest, then go ahead and do your thing, girl. But don't let the shiny things and the smooth talkers and the people selling you a dream distract you from what is really important in life. If there's one thing in life we never fail to take for granted, it's time. We never, ever have as much of it as we think.

So, yeah, go ahead and leave the nest if that's what feels right to you. Go ahead and start feeling yourself a little bit. I love that confidence. Spread those wings.

Live those dreams. You go ahead and soar, Black girls. You have my permission, but you don't need it. You've earned it.

Just do me a favor. Don't ever lose sight of who you really are, or where you came from, or the people who truly love you. You would be surprised at how fast the winds of life can change.

When you start to fall, who will be there to lift you up?

Your Day Ones. Your OGs. The people who were never afraid to tell you, *Yes, A'ja, your s*** do stink sometimes*.

Your people. Don't forget 'em.

Humbly,

A'ja Wil—

6

GRIEF DOESN'T CARE ABOUT YOUR NEAT LITTLE BOXES

Dear Black Girls,

This one is for the girls who are crying their eyes out every night.

This is for all the girls who don't feel like they can take a step out of bed in the morning.

This is for all the girls who don't even know what the point of life is anymore.

I know exactly how you feel.

The night I lost my grandmother, it felt like a part of my soul had died.

I can remember the pain like it was yesterday. It was around midnight. I was in the lobby of our dorm at South Carolina. It was the beginning of my sophomore year, and we were hosting a high school recruit for the weekend. That was always the best time because we were guaranteed to be eating good. We'd always take the recruit to Ruth's Chris Steak House and ball out. I was playing the role of Big Sis, naturally.

"See how we're living at SC? Go ahead and get yourself some crab cakes. Don't be shy, girl. This is SEC Basketball. Garçon? A ginger ale, please. WE DO IT BIG OUT HERE."

I had settled in after the natural butterflies of first year, and it felt like everything was falling into place for me. I knew the campus. I knew my teammates. My family was close by.

But then the minute I was feeling like I was in my cozy little comfort zone, my whole world fell apart.

All it took was one phone call.

When I got back to my dorm room that night, I was getting ready to go to bed when I saw that I had a missed call from my mom. That wasn't usual at all. We talked almost every day. But you know that uneasy feeling you get when your mom is calling you a little too late at night? I immediately called her back, wondering what was up. When she answered the call, she didn't even say hello.

She just said, "A'ja, you need to come downstairs."

I said, "What do you mean 'downstairs'? I'm in my room."

She said, "I know. Just come on downstairs, honey."

I said, "You're here? It's midnight. I'm in my bonnet. I look like a mess. What's going on?"

She said, "A'ja."

I went to my window and looked outside. My dad was there with her. It still didn't hit me. I was just confused. I walked down to the lobby and opened the door in sweatpants and my bonnet, and I remember I was kind of smiling. I was so naive. "What's up, guys? It's midnight. Y'all miss me that much?"

And then I remember my dad coming up to me and kind of holding me—almost like he knew I might collapse under the weight of the words to come. He grabbed my arms, and then my mom said, "Grandma passed tonight."

When I tell you I let out a scream . . .

I didn't think a person could scream that loud.

It came from the depths of my soul.

I woke up the entire dorm.

I was shaking.

I couldn't breathe.

All I can remember is my dad and my mom and my godmother surrounding me in this big huddle and holding me

as I screamed

and screamed

and screamed.

I just lost it.

I kept saying, "I want to see her. I want to go see her. Now."

My mom said, "She would want you to remember her the way she was, A'ja."

I said, "I need to go to the house at least. Take me to the house. Please, please take me to grandma's house."

So they put me into the car, and we drove right over to her house.

It is such an overwhelming feeling to walk in to a place you know so well—the smells, the furniture, the knickknacks, all the light switches, all the marks on the walls—when you walk in the door of that house and the person you love is gone, it's almost too much to process.

I can't describe the pain I felt, but at the same time, just being in that place that had given me so much love and nourishment my entire life . . . Whew. I felt such a powerful sense of gratitude and peace. I just sat there on her bed, and I could still smell her essence in that room, and I kept thinking: Thank you, Grandma. Thank you, thank you, thank you, thank you.

The connection we have can't be expressed in words. I can't do it in this paragraph, in this book, in this life. There are some emotions that go above and beyond language. Me and my grandma could just sit next to each other, not saying a word the whole time, and it was like my battery was charging up.

My soul would be getting filled up to the brim just by the waves of her presence.

With her gone, I literally did not know how I was going to go on.

When I woke up the next morning, life didn't seem to make any sense anymore.

Everything felt flat.

Food didn't taste the same.

Music didn't sound the same.

The sun didn't shine the same.

The only thought I had in my head was: *What's the point?*

Playing basketball? *What's the point? It's just a stupid game.*

School? *What's the point? What's the point of anything? Everything sucks.*

Everything I did up until that day—my motivation in the depths of my soul, if I'm being honest with myself— was to make my grandma proud. To put *my* little pins all over that plastic world map on her dining room table. To get my name in the newspaper so she could smile with her morning coffee. To bring her back her souvenir salt-n'-pepper shakers from all my road trips. I wanted to become the woman she always believed I could be. In her mind, I was always wearing a cape. She could see it on my shoulders even when I was a rambunctious little girl with no self-confidence. So I wanted to be that Superwoman, for her.

But now she was gone.

And so my reason for thriving was gone.

My WHY was gone.

That morning after she passed, I told my mom that I didn't want to play basketball anymore. She thought I was bluffing.

I went to my room and didn't come out until I had written a whole saga of a letter to Coach Staley explaining why I was quitting the team. All I wanted to do was lie in bed under a pile of blankets and cry. It's so amazing to me how powerful the scent of someone is when they're gone. My grandma used to knit quilts for everybody in the family, and I just buried my head in those quilts and tried to go back in time.

I did not want to accept reality.

I did not want to move on.

I wanted to bury myself in blankets and give up.

The thought of going to basketball practice just seemed totally ridiculous to me. I didn't even have the energy to tie my shoes, let alone run a fast break. I texted Coach Staley and told her I had to step away from the team, and that I had a letter I wanted to give her.

I remember Coach called me immediately. "A'ja, you take as much time as you need. But do not bring me that letter. I'm not reading it. I want to talk to you in person, whenever you're ready."

That night, she took the thirty-minute drive over to my parents' house and sat down with me while I grieved. I don't think I even said any words. I just cried my eyes out.

That was when Dawn Staley solidified herself as the greatest human being on earth to me. Not many college coaches would have sat there for hours with a nineteen-year-old sobbing and snotting on their shoulder. They would have been like, *Oh, I'm so sorry for your loss*, hopped in their car, and got the heck out of there before things got too personal.

But Dawn sat there with me, and she didn't even try to convince me to come back. She was just like, "It's hard. I'm not going to sugarcoat it. I know how much it hurts right now. Just take some time and think about what your grandma would want you to do. Whatever you decide to do, we're going to be here for you no matter what."

That meant the world to me. Dawn was really *seeing me* at that moment. She wasn't looking at me like her player. She wasn't looking at me like a problem to be managed. She was just hurting for me, and that was exactly what I needed.

Sometimes, all you need to say to someone is, "I know how much it hurts."

How can you ask for a better coach, or a better role model, than Dawn Staley?

She represents everything a Black woman should aspire to be:

She's strong, successful, and intelligent.

She's a boss.

She will not take an ounce of crap from anybody.

But she has never lost her empathy and compassion for people.

Dawn and the whole coaching staff even came to my grandma's funeral to pay their respects. That showed me it was so much bigger than basketball, for all of them. That team was not just my team. From that moment on, it was *family*.

When I was at my lowest moment, Dawn became

like a second mother to me—and I do not say that lightly. When I came back to school after the funeral, I had to dip my toe back into basketball little by little. I wish I could tell you I just prayed on it and flipped this switch, and I was able to channel all my grief and pain into basketball, but honestly?

That's not how grief works. Grief is a . . . *whew.* I can't even say the word I want to say and keep it PG-13!

Grief doesn't care about your timeline.

Grief doesn't care about your neat little boxes.

Grief is so messy.

Some days, I was really negative. Everything sucked. Everyone sucked. Basketball sucked. Life sucked.

There were a few times when I accidentally butt-dialed my grandma's number with my phone. When I realized what happened and saw her name pop up on the screen . . . When it really sank in that she was never going to be on the other end of that line again . . . I was broken for the rest of the day.

I couldn't function.

A lot of days, I was probably a miserable person to be around. It was just a dark, dark, dark time. The one thing that really saved me was uttering the three little words that are so hard for us to say as Black women.

I told Coach Staley, "I need help."

That was all she needed to hear. She got me hooked up with a good therapist, and we started talking. Shout-out to my therapists. Y'all are the real MVPs.

Mental health is something we can never talk about enough, especially in our community. I am a strong Black woman, and I have been talking to therapists since I was nineteen years old. Ain't no shame in it. As a matter of fact, it's the best decision I ever made. It's not like my therapist waved a magic wand or said some magic words and made everything alright. If anything, he helped me dive a little deeper into the pain and all the emotions that were swirling in my head every day. More than anything, he created a safe space for me where I can vent and feel vulnerable.

He just let a young, angry, confused Black woman talk. He never judged. He listened. (I wish more of y'all out there in the world would do the same.)

And listen, girls, I know some of you might be hearing the word *therapy* and thinking, "That's cool, but I got a homegirl I can talk to," or "I can always talk to my mom."

But sometimes, as much as you love and trust your family and friends and coaches, you hold back a little bit. There are things I've told my therapist that I've only shared with him.

Even after I ripped up the letter to Dawn telling her I wanted to quit basketball and rejoined the team, there were still so many times when I called my mom and told her, "I just can't do it anymore."

I know people look at me as this super-strong person and this champion, and this role model for women and girls and everything. So I'm here to tell you there were so many nights when I was just on my knees in my room, sniffing one of my grandma's quilts, so ready to give up.

Prayer was my only means of communicating with my grandma. I would just close my eyes and think about her so hard, and I would talk to her. I remembered she always used to tell my mom one thing over and over again, and the exact words of it didn't hit me until she was gone. The words are so important. Whenever I wasn't around, and it was just her and my mom, she would say, "A'ja is going to be special. She's going to make a huge impact."

Now, you have to remember . . . she didn't know anything about basketball. I don't even think she realized you could make a living playing it. She would tell my mom that way before I even started playing basketball, back when I was a nobody.

"A'ja is going to be special. She's going to make a huge *impact*."

The last part is what resonated with me so much. I remembered the coin I picked up from her bedside after she passed. I don't even know how it caught my eye. I was lying on her bed, just reminiscing, looking through the stuff on her bedside, when I saw this little gold coin.

I picked it up, and it said, "Be a servant of God."

That was my grandmother in a nutshell. You don't have to be religious to understand the power of those words. She lived a hard life. At the end, she was almost blind, and she couldn't speak, but just being in the room with her, you could feel her energy charging up your battery, filling up your soul.

She lived for others. She wanted to put a smile on their faces. She wanted to bring joy to your heart in her own quiet way. She was not a rich person or a famous person, but she was a humble servant of God. What better purpose can you have in life than to try to be of service to others? What better WHY?

Of all the things my grandma could have kept on her bedside as she left this world, she kept that coin there. It was like her final parting message to me.

A'ja, just be a servant.

Ever since that night, I've taken that coin with me everywhere I've gone in the world. It's been in my backpack for every road trip in college and every away game in the WNBA. I just tried to make it my mission to make my grandma proud of who I was as a person because she damn sure didn't care about how many points I put up. She always believed I was going to make an impact on the world, and so I made it my mission to prove her right. That became my new WHY. Just make a difference in somebody's day—even if it's a little bitty difference.

Now, don't get it twisted. I've had many, many, many bad days since I picked up that coin. In life, there are so many days when you'll want to just get off the dang roller coaster and give up. You'll want to crawl under your blankets and never come out again.

I am not a perfect person.

The version of me you see on Instagram? The version you see of me on billboards and TV commercials? It's just that—a version of me. Me at my best. But there's also the version of me who wakes up some mornings looking and feeling like a hot mess. Sometimes, I still get negative. Sometimes, I still have dark days. Sometimes, I still miss my grandma like crazy.

But when I was lost and without a purpose in life, that coin found me.

So, to all the girls who are struggling right now.

To all the girls who have lost someone.

To all the girls who don't want to climb out of bed in the morning.

Hey, I know how bad it hurts. I've been there. I'm not here to paint a pretty picture. It sucks. I know it.

But just because someone is gone from this world doesn't mean you can't talk to them. They are still out there—*trust me* on that.

And if you close your eyes and think hard about what they meant to you, I swear you will feel your battery charging up. You will feel their presence. You will hear their voice. And their words may even reach you louder than ever.

Love forever,

A'ja Wilson

7

DO NOT CHOMP THAT CHEESE

Dear Black Girls,

This one is for all the girls out there who work so dang hard to be great, but they still never call you "blue collar."

This is for all the girls out there who are so dominant that they have to label you a "bully."

This is for all the girls out there who can't even celebrate without it being "classless."

This is for all the Black girls out there who are winning so much that all the haters want is to see you lose.

Girls, this chapter is not for the faint of heart. But if you've come this far, then you know I'm always going to keep it raw and uncut. I got some bad news for you.

Don't worry; I got some good news, too! But let's start with reality. . . .

They *will* hit you with the okey doke. They *will* hit you with the double standard.

They *will* hit you with the outrageous labels. And some of them will do it with a smile.

I've lived on this earth for twenty-seven years now, and it's so wild to me how they label us. *Especially* when we're shining.

No matter how much success you have, or how well you treat people, or how far you climb up the rungs of that ladder, there will always—and I mean *always*—be people who want to take you down a few pegs.

There're two ways that people try to tear down Black women in this country.

There's the way you see it on social media, where it's just so in your face. You know all the vile comments I'm talking about. That's the nasty way, and it's almost easier to shrug that stuff off. I know that sounds crazy, but you get so used to seeing it, since these social media companies refuse to do anything about it, and it's all just so *stupid*, that you get numb to it. You may already feel numb to it.

But then there's another way they try to get to you. The slippery way. You know what I'm talking about.

They drag you with a smile on their face. They drag you down with a little wink. They drag you with a "What do you mean? Why are you getting so upset?"

For some reason, this way *really* bothers me.

I'll never forget walking through campus my first year at South Carolina and seeing some girls I went to high school with, getting hit with the super-surprised, "A'ja??? A'ja *Wilson???* What are *you* doing here?"

I'm thinking, "What am *I* doing here? I'm going to class. What are *you* doing here?"

I mean, remember: I was the number-one high school recruit in the country. I had boxes of letters from hundreds of schools. I hate talking about myself like this, but come on, girl! My decision made national news! You know exactly what I'm doing here!

I said, "I go here."

She's like, "Oh, that's cool. We didn't even know you applied."

I mean, it's 8:00 a.m., and she's testing me with the passive-aggressive nice stuff. It's too early for this, Lord! I didn't even know how to respond. In my head, I'm thinking, "Girl, I didn't apply anywhere. I'm here on a scholarship. I worked my tail off to get here. Didn't you see those ESPN cameras rolling up to our high school last year?"

But I was raised to always turn the other cheek, so I just smiled back and hit her with the "Yyyeaaahhh, guuuurllll. OK! So great to see you! Take care now! Byyyeeee!"

To this day, I literally do not know if she was purposely being a hater or if she just couldn't imagine we could possibly be going to the same university. Honestly, I don't think she had bad intentions. It's more subtle than that. It's like a reflex. It's like all she could see was the A'ja Wilson who struggled in writing class, or the A'ja Wilson who needed her special pen that recorded the teacher's lessons in class. She could only see the A'ja Wilson who was beneath her.

That was my first hint that no matter how brightly I shined or how big of a name I made for myself, there were always going to be people who saw me walk into a room and thought, *Wait, what is* she *doing here?*

A few months later, that same person was probably hitting me up on Facebook for tickets to a game. The thing people don't understand about our experience as Black women is we have to bear so much of this nonsense with a smile on our face. Because if we dare to react?

Girls, I don't have to tell you what's going to happen. You have probably already experienced it a hundred times.

"Why are you getting so upset?"

"Why are you overreacting?"

"Why are you so emotional?"

For every emotion you want to have as a human being, they will have a label ready to slap on you.

Who is "they"?

It's not everybody. But They are out there. Go on Twitter, or look in IG comments, or turn on the television, and They will be in your face. The more you accomplish, the more They will want to bring you down. I know because I lived it firsthand.

They came for me, and They will come for you, too.

But I got some good news for you, I promise. Let me just tell you a story.

When I first came to South Carolina, there were no expectations for the women's basketball program. Literally, when Dawn Staley was recruiting me, she was like, "Well, I'm going to be honest. I don't have much to offer you. But we're building something here, and I have a plan."

South Carolina had never won the SEC tournament. Never made a Final Four. But Dawn wasn't kidding. She was definitely building something special, and we made our first Final Four my first year. We started packing our arena, setting all kinds of attendance records. All of a sudden, our team was getting a lot of attention.

But what's so special about Coach Staley is she never lost sight of the fact that she was a Black woman coaching a team of Black girls in the South. Even when things were going really well for us, and it seemed like it was nothing but positive vibes for us, she banned us from using social media during the season. I remember she would let us reinstall Instagram for one weekend between the SEC Tournament and March Madness. Then we had to shut it down again.

I remember thinking she was just being a meanie.

"Come on, Coach. Why can't I be on Snapchat? Let me live, lady!!!"

But Dawn could see the bigger picture. She knew how toxic social media could be, especially for young Black women. She was protecting us from the darkness that we were too naive to see at the time. We were winning, so we thought everybody loved us. She was in rooms we weren't in, and she heard the comments and the labels we couldn't hear. She knew there were snakes in our own backyard.

For me, that protection was so key. Looking back on it now, I was fragile. I mean, I was still a *kid*. Even before my grandmother's death, I would constantly be coming into Coach Staley's office crying my eyes out over some dumb nineteen-year-old drama.

"Coach, I can't practice today."

"What's going on, A'ja?"

"I just . . ."

"A'ja, what's wrong?"

"Girl, why isn't he texting me back? I just don't get it!"

"A'ja."

"Why is he ghosting me, Coach? WHY??? It doesn't even make any sense."

"A'ja, take some tissues from the box, and go and put your practice gear on."

"Coach."

"A'ja, can I be honest with you?"

"Yeah, Coach. Yeah." (Sobbing.)

"You were a dumbass for pining over that dumbass boy. He's a zero. You're one in a million. Don't be silly. The answer is right in front of you. Leave his dumb ass."

(Sniffling.) "You right, Coach. You right. You so right."

"We good? Now let's go practice."

Dawn helped me channel that raw emotion of being a young woman into the game of basketball. She showed me how to use it as an outlet for everything: frustration, fear, anger, pain, insecurity. There were some nights when I went out and dropped twenty-five points in a game just because some dumbass boy was ghosting me.

You can laugh if you want, but when you're a young woman, this stuff seriously affects you.

Love is a terrible drug, let me tell you! And for some reason, it's the only drug we all willingly take.

I can't even imagine how hard it must be for girls now. I'm low-key aging myself here, but I was going through all this before Hinge and Bumble and all the dating apps came out. (Hold on, let me put on my granny glasses). Back in my day, you had to put in *work* to shoot your shot. When those new basketball, football, and soccer rosters dropped, that was like Christmas. We were going through the list, like, "Ohh, that name sounds cute. Hey, look him up on Facebook. Lemme see a profile pic real quick." You'd be out here sending friend requests, trying to see what was up.

Now all you gotta do is swipe right? *Shoot.* That's a piece of cake.

But I know that we had it easier in a lot of ways, too. During the last ten years, social media and all these apps have only made it harder for young women. The vibes are just so . . . harsh. I can't imagine being eighteen, nineteen, twenty years old now and dealing with so much negativity. It feels like we made the whole *world* a middle school cafeteria. Every single table is the mean girls' table, and you can hear every single thing those girls are saying behind your back. It's not even being whispered, like in the movies—they're out here screaming to your face.

I was shielded from so much of this nonsense, and I was *still* crying my eyes out in Dawn's office at least once a week.

Thank God for Dawn Staley, for real.

There are so many things you go through as a Black woman that only another Black woman can understand on a deep, *deep* level. That's no shots at the white coaches out there. I know many of them care about their players, and are there for them through thick and thin, but with me and Dawn, it was just different. There were times when I could just shoot her a *look* from across the room, and she would know exactly what I was going through. I wouldn't even have to say a word. There would be times in practice when I was trying to hide it, but she would call me into her office and say, "A'ja, I know you're going *through it* right now. I can feel it in your aura. You can't hide from me. What's going on?"

I needed Dawn Staley in my life, especially after I lost my grandma. She could understand my daily struggle in a different way. There would be some days when, out of the blue, I just could not get out of my head. Coach would call me into her office, and I'd be like, "There's nothing wrong, Coach. I don't know. I just *miss her*, that's all."

As a young woman, all you want is to be seen and heard by somebody else. Dawn Staley saw me. And don't get me wrong, Coach was not a softy. Dawn Staley is *Philly* through and through. When we were on the court, she would be calling my ass out in front of the entire team if she thought I was mailing it in. There were days when she would be like, "Hey, 22! Get 22 off the floor! Get her out of the gym! She doesn't deserve to be here!"

She wasn't joking. She would literally kick me out of the gym.

I would come into her office with my hands up in the air, shaking my head, tears welling up in my eyes.

She'd say, "You were blending in. You're a star. You need to be taking over. If I see you out there blending in, fading into the background, *hiding?* I'm kicking you out of the gym."

That's the thing about Dawn Staley, and about all great mentors. They defy an easy explanation. Dawn let me cry on her shoulder. She let me vent. She let me grieve. She protected me from the evils of the world. But she also challenged me to be great.

She knew the score. She knew she was coaching the number-one team in the country. She knew we had a chance to make history for the program. She knew that, right now, when everything is smooth sailing, and we're selling out our building, and people have their Gamecocks flags flying in their front yards—some of them even flying right next to Confederate flags?

It's all good, for now. Everybody loves us, for now.

But she also knew she was coaching a team of Black girls in the South—no, don't even worry about the South. A team of Black girls in the *world*. We hated her for blocking us from social media. We hated her for making us work twice as hard as every other team. We hated her for harping on the smallest mistakes—mistakes that didn't even matter when we were up twenty points. We hated her for treating us like we needed to be protected.

And now, we love her for it.

Because we did have to work twice as hard as everyone else.

We did have to be dang-near close to perfect.

We did have to be protected.

We were a bunch of successful, young Black women with a spotlight on us. I can't think of a more dangerous combination. It was only a matter of time before they set up the Mouse Trap.

Y'all don't know about the Mouse Trap?

The whole world saw it play out during the 2023 Women's Final Four with the whole Caitlin Clark versus Angel Reese controversy. For those who don't remember, or who were smart enough to ignore the noise: Angel Reese caused the dumbest fake "controversy" of 2023 because she celebrated at the end of the championship game by doing the "You Can't See Me" gesture to her opponent Caitlin Clark (Oh, Lord, just google it). She also pointed to her ring finger, like, *Hey, we the champs*.

It was just run-of-the-mill, heat-of-the-moment trash talk.

Except, of course, a young Black woman did it.

For an entire week, every single media organization in America started acting like they followed women's basketball. All of a sudden, CNN and Fox News have us front and center? All of a sudden, we're headline news? All of a sudden, everybody has an opinion on two young female hoopers? What changed?

Y'all already know what changed.

When an opportunity presented itself to pit a white player against a Black player on the national stage, the media couldn't wait to exploit it. It was a setup from the jump. You could see it in the way both teams were framed in the coverage leading up to the final. They run the same playbook year after year. Look at the terms they use. Iowa was framed as the scrappy underdog. They were the blue-collar team. And what was LSU? They were the team that was going to "bully" you. They were the "athletes." They were going to turn the game into a "street fight."

If you didn't know better, you would've thought LSU was a No. 1 seed and Iowa was a No. 10 seed, when in reality LSU was the 3 and Iowa was the 2. The way the narrative around the game was framed, it was the big bad Black girls versus the scrappy, hard-nosed white girls, and they didn't have to hit you over the head with it. They did it in a subtle way. They did it with labels.

It's no surprise emotions boiled at the end of that final. Basketball is already an emotional game, but when you have the media stoking the fires, pitting a bunch of young women against one another in such a blatant and disrespectful way, then you *already know* what's going to happen.

They set the mouse trap.

And they had the whole country chompin' on the cheese.

Angel Reese gave Caitlin Clark a bit of her own medicine back to her with the "You Can't See Me" gesture, and America lost its collective dang mind.

If you've ever played a game of basketball in your life, let alone a pro game, with real stakes, on the national stage, then you've seen this kind of thing a thousand times. When a white girl celebrates like this, it's confidence. It's swagger. It's that killer competitiveness. "Oh, she's got that Mamba Mentality."

But when a Black girl does the same thing, now it's cockiness. Now it's disrespectful. Now it's a whole bunch of words that I will not repeat here.

When a white girl's doing it, it's cute.

When a Black girl's doing it, it's a crisis.

Chomp that cheese.

And I want to be clear. It's not like our white counterparts are asking for any of this. They are set up for the okey doke just like we are. You can see it in the way that the media tried to corner Caitlin Clark after the game. All year, the media built her up as the hero, and now she's got to stand up on that podium and solve all of America's problems? How is that fair to her?

Then you got another twenty-one-year-old girl, Angel Reese, who just experienced all her dreams coming true, and when she gets back to the locker room and picks up her phone, she's being bombarded with death threats and racist messages.

All over a game of basketball.

114

This is the mouse trap. It's just the way the entire internet works now, and it's *sick*. To the world, it's just clicks and likes and drama.

But these are their *lives*.

You are playing around with these young women's lives for your entertainment. It has to stop.

This is so personal to me because I lived through this same script at South Carolina back in 2017. In a lot of ways, it was the best year of my life. We were on our way to making history. First SEC trophy. First Final Four berth. First national championship in school history.

We didn't add to the trophy case. We *built* the trophy case. And you would have thought it was nothing but positivity. But, honestly, when I look back on that time, I remember one thing most of all.

They never let us forget who we were.

We were the Black girls. Always.

We were aggressive. We were cocky. We were the big bad bullies. We were whatever fit the narrative that day. We were never the underdogs, even when we were the underdogs. Even when we've been the underdogs our whole lives.

We were shielded from so much of the negativity by Coach Staley. She kept us in our little bubble. She was our rock. She was our shoulder to cry on. I don't understand how she could be so unflappable. We would try to push her buttons so many times, just to see if we could get a reaction out of her, but you could never get this woman to crack. She was cool as a cucumber.

I didn't even understand how much of the burden she was taking on her shoulders until years later, when I was already in the WNBA, and I was talking to another coach. That was when they told me the truth.

"Some of the emails and the messages she gets, you simply wouldn't believe. The world is a cruel place, and she shielded you girls from all of that."

Without Coach Staley, the world would have probably eaten me alive. Without her, I would have never come out of my room after my grandmother's death. I was ready to walk away from the game. I was ready to give up on life.

Now, listen: Our relationship was not all sunshine and rainbows. I'm going to keep it real with you. Half the time, she probably wanted to kill me.

There were so many times I came into her office and told her, "I quit! I'm ready to transfer! I hate it here!"

There were so many times when she had to yell, "Get 22 out of my gym!"

There were so many times when she had to tell me I was being a dumbass *because I was being a dumbass.*

But then there were so many times when she reminded me of my worth as a Black woman, when it seemed like the whole world wanted to tear me down.

There were so many times when she told me to ignore the comments, delete the app—*Hell, girl, shut your whole phone off. Why do you care what these losers think, anyway? You are A'JA WILSON. You are going to be something SPECIAL.*

There were so many times when she could have just been a coach to me, but she was a second mom instead.

Black girls, I am not here to sell you a dream.

The fact is, it's 2024, and they are still setting up that mouse trap. And it's not just in basketball. It's not just in sports. Whether you're a student or a lawyer or a teacher or a nurse or anything under the sun, they are going to frame the narrative a certain way.

When they celebrate, it's confidence.

When you celebrate, it's cockiness.

When they talk trash, it's cute.

When you talk trash, it's a crime.

When they cry in front of the cameras, it's passion.

When you cry in front of the cameras, it's a meme.

It's not fair, and it's probably not changing any time soon. There's always going to be a certain segment of the world that simply does not want to see a bunch of young Black girls shining.

I know that's hard to comprehend. I know you want to *fix it*. I know you want to defend yourself. But you can't reason with those people. You can't reach their hearts. That's up to them and God.

But lucky for us, there's a light at the end of the tunnel. I told you I had some good news for you. I lived it, so you can trust me.

See . . .

There's one label they can't just slap on to fit a narrative. There's one they can't fake. There's one that only sticks if it's actually *true*.

"Winner."

So keep on winning, Black girls.

Keep on striving.

Keep on shining.

I *see* you.

Mic drop,

A'ja Wilson

8

ALWAYS MEASURE YOUR DRESS SITTING DOWN

Dear Black Girls,

This one is for the independent young women out there in the real world for the first time.

This is for all the girls who are seeing those first direct deposits hit.

This is for all the sisters who are stepping into the spotlight.

OK, sit down. Take a few deep breaths, and do me a quick favor. Google a picture of me where I'm looking really dope. Like, maybe a picture of me holding up the SEC championship trophy with my bubblegum pink nails, cheesing on all the haters from Mississippi State. Or maybe a picture of me looking fly on a red carpet or something. Anything cute works.

Whatever you do, just please remember I can be cool. I have my moments.

Because I'm about to tell y'all a story so embarrassing that you're covered for the rest of your life. You're good, I swear. Anytime you feel embarrassed about something you said or did, all you have to do is remember what your girl A'ja did on the biggest night of her life.

No, it's bad, y'all.

If you feel like you put your foot in your mouth with your crush or whatever, all you gotta do is repeat these words like your own personal mantra: "I am not A'ja Wilson on Draft Night 2018. I am not A'ja Wilson on Draft Night 2018. It's not that bad. I am OK."

It all started off so good, too. I knew I was going to be the number-one pick. All my dreams were about to come true.

My family was going to be by my side. In New York City. We made it, y'all. All the way from Columbia, South Carolina, to the W. Let's GOOO!

It was such a full-circle moment for me and my family that I wanted to make sure we incorporated something in my draft night outfit to honor my grandmother. And girls, you know how it is on these kinds of nights. I knew the spotlight was going to be on me. I knew the trolls were going to be out in full force if I had even a little bitty *nail* chipped or a hair out of place.

Plus, my body type is not exactly "normal." I'm six-foot-five. I can't just roll up to Macy's and get something off the rack. So me and my mom found a designer, and I started sketching out some ideas. I knew it was going to be a long night, and they were going to be putting me through the media wringer, so I'm like, It's jumpsuit season. We rompin'. We rollin'. Easy breezy. Perfect.

The designer even found an amazing way to incorporate pearls into the design. If you've ever seen me on a basketball court in college, I was always rocking my pearls during warm-ups. They were a gift from the legendary Hattie Rakes, naturally. You know how grandmas just got those old-school sayings? When I was young, she was always saying, "Pretty girls wear pearls."

I'd be like, "Grandma, you crazy."

But then when I grew up and she gave me my first set of pearls, I was like, "Grandma, you're so dope. I'm never taking these off."

I just kind of made it my thing. Especially after my grandma passed, that was my way of remembering her when I went onto the court. I guess it was almost like a little piece of armor. I drew a lot of strength from those pearls. So we had to make sure they were part of my dress on Draft Night.

We go to the fitting. NO PROBLEMS. Romper fits like a glove. Beautiful blush-colored silk. Pearls worked

into the waistband. We're looking at it from every an-
gle. Looking in the full-length mirror. Taking pictures.
Perfect. I'm even feeling myself a little bit. I'm like,
Oh, they're gonna love this. Haters will be silenced.
Body-shamers will be crying. We did it. And! And! (As
a woman, you can't forget about every if, and, or but.)
And! This is not going to age poorly, either. I'm not about
to be out here looking like these 2003 NBA Draft dudes in
their XXL suits. No, no, no. I'm not about to be a meme
in twenty years. This is classy. This is classic. We are
golden.

Take one more look in the mirror. Check. One less
thing to stress about.

(Can you hear the horror movie music starting to
play real softly in the background?)

Draft Night rolls around, and the WNBA folks have
us running around New York the whole day. We're at
the Empire State Building. We're eating pizza. Photo
shoots. Interviews. Rookie orientation. It's just a whirl-
wind. So we get back to the hotel, and everybody is
supposed to be AT THE BUS to the draft at 6:25 p.m.
Bus leaves at 6:30 p.m. sharp.

My mom was telling me the whole day: "A'ja! Listen
to your mother. Do not be getting ready fifteen minutes
before the bus leaves."

So I start getting ready seventeen minutes before the bus leaves.

Outfit: Check. Hair: Check. Now, let's get these shoes on. And, girls, you know the move when you're getting dressed for something fancy in the hotel. You sit on the toilet seat to strap into your heels. So I go to sit down and . . .

Nope.

I'm like a cat who got a furball.

I make a noise like: "Kaaahhhh!"

Nope.

I cannot breathe.

This thing is too tight. I am getting choked by my own dress.

I stand back up. *Phew*. What in the world?

I sit back down.

"Kahhhh!"

Nope! Nope, nope, nope.

This dress is about to kill me. Picture this in your mind: The back of this jumpsuit is connected by an elegant . . . I don't know the term . . . let's just call it a neck-strap thingy. But every time I go to sit down, the fabric on my behind stretches, and the neck-strap thingy tightens.

My choker is choking me, for real.

Then the realization hits me.

Oh, my gosh. We did not measure this thing sitting down. We were only ever standing up. Oh, my gosh. Oh, my Lord.

I am going to be sitting down for two hours.

With TV cameras on me.

I'm the number-one pick.

We have a problem.

Oh, my Lord.

Lemme try one more. . . .

NOPE!!!!

At this moment, I can hear Diamond DeShields yelling for me in the other room. They had us rooming together. She was another top-five pick, and so, of course, she was super-duper hyped for the night. She's ready to rock! She's like, "A'ja, the bus is gonna leave us!"

Now I'm panicking. And whenever I panic, you already know the first person I'm calling. I pick up my phone.

"Mom, we got a problem!"

"A'ja, we're all down here in the lobby ready to take pictures. Where are you?"

"Mom, I just need you."

"What?"

"I just *need* you!"

You know when it's so bad that all you can say is, *Mom, I just* need *you*???

At this point, I'm lying down in the empty bathtub with my feet up on the ledge, just trying to get the straps on any way I can. My mom walks in, and I'm like, "Help, Momma! Help! This choker is choking me."

Between me, her, and Diamond, we finally get me into my heels and back on my feet again, and the whole time, my mom is just grumbling—she's not even yelling, just grumbling to herself: "I told her. Don't I always tell her? Fifteen minutes. I told her."

We run out to the bus, and I am just praying: "Lord, please do not let me rip the seat of this romper on national television."

The entire bus ride to the draft, I am shifting in my seat, trying to stand up a little bit to get a breath. Literally, if that bus ride had been ten minutes longer, I think I would have passed out. All the other draftees are just looking at me like, *Is this girl OK? Is she just nervous? What the heck is going on?*

We finally get to the red carpet (actually, orange carpet for the W), and all the media is there, and everyone is asking me, "Oh, my gosh, who are you wearing? Your dress is so beautiful."

I'm just smiling, trying to fake it, but in the back of my mind, I'm thinking: *I am really about to become a meme. This is so bad. How do I get out of this? Can I fake being sick? Can I find a way to stand up the whole time? Do I act like I'm cramping up? LORD, SHOW ME THE WAY.*

They put us all in this greenroom before the TV cameras start rolling, and you can just imagine the tension, excitement, nerves, and everything. You got all these women whose lives are about to change. Literally the biggest moment of their entire lives.

And then you got A'ja Wilson sitting down in this chair, leaning way back, legs sprawled out like a dude who is living in his mom's basement with a beer in his hand, playing video games or something. All my girls are looking at me like, *What is happening right now? Are we being pranked?*

Finally, I had to tell them my situation. I said, "Listen, y'all. Can I just be real with you? I got a little wardrobe malfunction going on right now. I didn't measure this dress sitting down. I can't breathe if I sit up straight."

I remember someone was like, "Well, you're going number one, so you only got, like, twenty minutes to sit there. I think you can make it."

They were all really cool about it. Everybody had *been there* before, you know? If you're a woman, then you know that feeling.

We finally got out to the main room with all the families and everything, and we cleared out one whole side of our table and set it up so the tablecloth was covering my legs. I hiked the jumpsuit up super high, and I was literally leaning back with my legs butterflied out under my mom's chair like I was giving birth.

If you watch the broadcast back, when the Las Vegas Aces announce me as their number-one pick, you can see me leaning way back in my chair, stiff as a board, almost like I'm too cool for school. But all I was thinking was, "Lord, thank you, thank you, thank you. Let me get this oxygen. I am never sitting down again."

Thank God I went number one because if I'd gone number two, I would have been blue.

Holly Rowe, one of the biggest ESPN reporters, was interviewing me, asking me what the moment meant to me, and I couldn't even think straight.

I think I said something about overcoming adversity in college, and how much my parents sacrificed to get me on that stage, but I should have grabbed the microphone, stared straight into the camera, and said, "GIRLS ALL ACROSS THE WORLD. THIS IS A

PUBLIC SERVICE ANNOUNCEMENT. LISTEN TO ME. ALWAYS MEASURE YOUR DRESS SITTING DOWN. *ALWAYS*. MEASURE. IT. SITTING. DOWN."

You can laugh if you want to, but this is the side of being a young woman in the spotlight that we don't let y'all see. For so much of our lives, when we're supposed to be soaking up the moment, all we can think about is: Is my dress about to rip? Do my nails look OK? Do I got the resting b-face going? Should I smile more? I'm hungry; I don't feel like smiling. I gotta smile. Dang, I hope my hair isn't looking crazy with this humidity.

I envy the women who can stay out of their heads about this stuff, but we all know the game. If we slip up, even for one hot second? They're going to be all up in your IG comments, mean-girling, *mean-guying* you.

Sir, you're a forty-five-year-old man with two daughters. Why are you taking time out of your day to talk about my hair?

And, ma'am! You got your granddaughter in your profile picture, and you really took time out of your day just to comment: Guess she didn't have time to get her nails done??? Laughing emoji-laughing emoji-facepalm emoji.

It's sad, but that's the reality for us as Black women.

We are being judged twenty-four seven, even by our own community. So on the biggest night of my life, when I should have been soaking in the moment, I was just trying not to show the world my butt, literally.

Everything from me putting on my jumpsuit to me hugging my parents was a blur. I think the moment that it all really sank in for me was when I saw Dawn Staley backstage.

That was really a We Did It moment.

Not an I Did It.

We Did It.

Now, let me be clear: Dawn Staley annoyed the *hell* out of me for four years. But she really was a second mom to me, and I never would have seen my dreams come true without her. Giving her that hug as a certified WNBA player was so emotional, but I had to tell her, "Girl, I can't bend down too far, or else we're going to have a real problem."

Now, you might be asking yourself why I am even telling this embarrassing story in the first place. Is the point that you always need to measure your dress sitting down? Not really.

Is the point that you need to listen to your mom and stop getting dressed seventeen minutes before you're about to leave? Not really.

Is the point that you need to be able to laugh at yourself? Not really, but it helps.

The real point, Black girls, is you don't know what you don't know. There's going to be so many experiences in your life that are new to you, and you're going to be in rookie mode, and you may even embarrass yourself a little bit sometimes, and that's OK.

We don't grow up with a perfect handbook to life. For a lot of us, we're the first people in our families to experience certain things. It's funny because when I was a kid, I looked at the legends of women's basketball, like Diana Taurasi or Lisa Leslie, and thought once you get to that level, your life is gravy. They got it all figured out, right? Nobody can tell them nothin'. They probably don't even sweat. (I definitely couldn't picture them lying in a hotel bathtub struggling to put on heels thirty minutes before the WNBA Draft.)

The irony is the more you achieve in life, and the older you get, and the more experiences you have, the more you start thinking: *I actually don't know a dang thing.*

What am I doing here?

Who let me in this place?

They must have made a mistake.

Somebody CALL MY MOM.

This is why I don't like the term *impostor syndrome*.

It's almost like we are taught there's something wrong with these emotions, when they're actually just a part of life.

On the basketball court, I knew I belonged. Shoot, I knew I was *good*, don't get it confused. But I was also a young woman who moved all the way across the country from South Carolina to Vegas for a new job with a whole bunch of people I'd never met before and a whole lot of pressure and expectations. Everything was new. The city, the facilities, the culture, and just the way of life.

I'll never forget the first time I was driving around the Strip in Vegas. I was all alone in my car, and I just genuinely started panicking because people were driving *crazy*—or at least crazy to my nice and polite South Carolinian mind. I didn't know where I was going, and the GPS was telling me I had to change lanes, and nobody would let me over. In South Carolina, we will brake to let you in and even toss in a little friendly *Come On Over* wave with a smile and some Southern charm.

I'm sorry, but that's just being a good neighbor, OK?

In Vegas, they were speeding up just to keep me *boxed out*. It felt personal, y'all. Spiteful. I lost it. I started literally crying in the car, and I called my mom in a panic, like, "Mom, ohmygod, ohmygod what is HAPPENING! I don't know what to do."

She's like, "What are you talking about? Where are you?"

I'm like, "I'm on the highway. And . . . the traffic! And! These people! I just . . . And . . ."

She said, "A'ja, you need to pull yourself together."

I said, "I don't know where I'm going. You need to come out here. This is crazy."

And then she hit me with the Certified Mom Classic. You know this one.

"A'ja Wilson. You are twenty-two years old. You live in Las Vegas now. We live in South Carolina. I am not flying across the country every time somebody won't let you change lanes. You are a grown-ass woman. You can do this."

Cars are zooming by me. I'm going, like, twenty-five miles an hour.

"Mom! Help!"

"A'ja. You're a big girl. Listen to the nice GPS lady."

Click.

I think I cried all the way back to my apartment, but I made it. My mom knows me better than anyone, and she knew I wasn't having a meltdown over navigating some highway. It was about navigating a new world.

There were so many times during my rookie year when I just felt so out of my element—not as a basketball player, but as a human. Like I was the first Black woman in history ever to leave home and live on her own and start her first job.

All I did, every single day, was go to practice, and then come back to my apartment and watch *The Office*. I was in full-on Loner Mode. Curtains pulled. Shades down. Y'all going *out?* Cool. I'm staying *in*. All I'm trying to do is chill with Michael Scott and hydrate in my nice little cozy cave.

You can never appreciate these things in the moment, but looking back on it, those times were so important.

You need to be able to feel a little bit lonely.

You need to be able to feel a little bit lost.

You need to *feel things*.

Part of growing up—*really* growing up—is slowly getting comfortable with being uncomfortable.

Mom isn't always going to be there to do your laundry, or make sure you don't start getting ready seventeen minutes before you have to leave, or tell you when you're putting your foot in your mouth. The only way you can learn those things is by going through those awkward, lonely, frustrating, embarrassing, crying-your-mascara-all-over-your-face moments.

Sometimes, you may even have to put your foot in your mouth just to remember how it tastes.

If you're like me, you may even do it in front of the entire world.

July 1, 2018. Right in the middle of my rookie year. I'm finally starting to get comfortable. My parents had come out to visit me, and I'm sitting with my dad, having some dinner at this café right across the street from the Staples Center.

I'm on my phone, like usual. Reading the tweets, like usual. Mindlessly scrolling. Then I see the news LeBron James had just signed his big contract with the Lakers. A cool $154 million. And A'ja being A'ja, my fingers started typing out a tweet before my brain even caught up with me. No filter. Just vibes. I tweeted out:

154M . . . . must. be. nice. We over here looking for a M 😊. But Lord, let me get back in my lane.

I attached a cute little GIF. Bang. Fired it off. Not thinking anything of it. My only point was just: Hey, wouldn't it be great if they invested in our league with a fraction of this money, so we could see how it would grow?

THE LEAST HOT TAKE EVER.

So I go back to my salad or whatever. Who cares about what A'ja Wilson is saying, right?

Girls, two rules: Do not be drinking and driving, and do not be tweeting and eating. You are not in full control of all your faculties.

Two minutes later, I'm talking to my dad about W stuff, and my phone starts vibrating. It starts really small at first, like the group chat is going crazy. I let it go. Let me finish this food.

But then it keeps getting more and more frequent.

Then, it's buzzing nonstop.

I thought it was a glitch or something.

I pick up the phone, and it's just nonstop Twitter notifications. That bird was chirping. I'm like: *OK, this is never good*.

I look at my replies, and the LeBron Stans were up in arms. They were coming for me. I will not even go into the worst ones, but a lot of the vibe was: "What is this woman talking about? What gives her the right? What an idiot."

Hundreds and hundreds of comments. There were also a lot of people who were dialed in to what I was saying who were supporting me, but it just turned into this firestorm on both sides, and I was shaking.

I showed my dad my phone and was like, "Oh, my God, did I just disrespect LeBron James? He is definitely going to see this, isn't he? Am I in trouble? The King is gonna hate me—Oh, Lord."

As a young woman, and especially as a young Black woman, these moments can leave you legitimately shook. Some of the comments can be vile and downright violent, and you know it's just some words on a screen—but when you're living it, it's not just words on a screen.

I remember my dad being like, "I'm old. I don't understand this stuff. Can't you just ignore them? They're strangers, right?"

I'm like, "Dad, they're writing news stories about it now!"

He's like, "They're writing news stories about your text message?"

"Dad! You don't get it!"

I remember reading one of the most horrible comments and clicking on the guy's profile, and it literally read: FATHER OF TWO DAUGHTERS.

I mean . . . sir!

Sir!!!!

I really thought I was about to be canceled, y'all. Who comes at the King as a twenty-two-year-old rookie? I was so embarrassed. After trying to keep my head down and not make a peep my whole rookie year, I fired off one tweet while eating a Greek salad and went viral for all the wrong reasons.

I was thinking: *Just keep your mouth shut, A'ja. Nobody wants to hear what you have to say. Just go hoop and go home and watch* The Office.

But then a few months later, something crazy happened. I got this email, and I couldn't even believe what I was seeing. LeBron James was about to drop his new shoe at this big Nike event in Harlem, and as part of the show, he was going to honor eighteen women who represented strength and prowess in their fields.

The list was a bunch of superwomen. Serena Williams. Simone Biles. Lena Waithe. Maya Moore.

A'ja Wilson.

A'ja Wilson???

A'JA WILSON!!!!

Had to be a typo.

I had to look four or five times to make sure I was not hallucinating.

Lebron James had honored me with the title, "Rookie with a Voice."

I can't tell you how much that meant to me. Not as

a basketball player. As a human being. As a twenty-two-year-old in a new city, in a new job. As somebody who felt like she had put her foot in her mouth and who got her hand slapped for speaking up at all. That was one of the biggest superstars in the world saying, "Nah. I see you. I hear you. I *got* you. Your words are powerful."

That was the moment when I really found my voice.

That tweet hadn't been a mistake at all. It was just A'ja being A'ja. My filter *been* broken since I was six years old. Why fix it now?

The pay gap between the men and women *is* ridiculous. Listen, $154 million is absurd when our superstars are just trying to get one single itty-bitty M. Why would I be silent when I can stand up? Because it's polite? Because it's LeBron?

I can only be me, even if it pisses off half of America.

That little viral moment and LeBron's reaction to it made me realize all my awkward moments and my weird little jokes and all the growing pains I thought were problems—they weren't problems at all.

They were what made me a real person, and a real force.

Black girls, you will make mistakes.

You will do embarrassing things. You will put your

foot in your mouth. You will split your fit. You will cry in traffic. You will piss off a PROUD FATHER OF TWO DAUGHTERS.

You will do all kind of things that aren't "perfect."

My advice: Keep doing 'em. Keep standing up. Keep being you.

Life ain't about perfection. It's about progress.

Imperfectly,

Aja Wil—

PS: *Seriously, measure that dress sitting down though, for real.*

9

IT'S OK TO BE NOT OK

Dear Black Girls,

This one is for the girls out there who feel like they can hardly breathe.

This is for all the girls out there who feel like they have the weight of the world on their chests.

This is for all the girls who are simply not OK right now.

I need you to really hear me for a minute. I need you to *feel* this.

If you're here for smiling A'ja, or perfect A'ja, or curated A'ja, then I don't have anything for you.

I'm just warning everybody from the jump. You know what? I'll even give you an easy way out: If you don't feel like getting deep today, then just roll on over to the next chapter.

Or better yet, shut this book right now and head on over to @acendeuce_. (Yes, that's acendeuce plus an underscore.) That's the Instagram account for my two adorable Aussiepoos. They are always up to some whimsical shenanigans. Guaranteed to lift your spirits. I'm not bragging, but LET A MOM BRAG, OK?

If you're not feeling it today, I won't hold it against you.

But for everybody who wants the *real* A'ja, I will give it to you straight.

Four years ago, I had my first panic attack. I really thought I was about to die.

I was on vacation with my whole family down at Kiawah Island, off the coast of South Carolina. We were in the car driving to the outlet malls. Nothing better than some deep-discount athleisure, am I right? Bright, sunny day. Off-season vibes. Surrounded by love.

But for some reason, my anxiety was *humming*. That's the only way I can describe it.

My brain would not chill.

My chest started getting tighter and tighter—and it was little by little, almost like a snake was slowly wrapping itself around me. That was when I really started to spiral, when I had that fleeting thought: *Am I able to breathe right now?*

My dad was driving, and I was sitting there having a conversation with him and my mom, but my whole body started to get numb. It felt like my chest was caving in.

My hands got tingly and cold.

Heart was pumping like crazy.

It felt like the walls of the car were literally closing in on me. But it was even scarier than that. The best way I can describe it is my entire *world* started to feel like it was getting really, really small. In my head, I'm like, *Am I having a heart attack? I'm twenty-four years old. Can twenty-four-year-olds have heart attacks? Because I feel like I'm having a f******* heart attack.*

I tell my dad, "Hey, I'm not feeling good. I don't know what's—"

And then I just started throwing up. Right in the car. Everywhere.

My dad had to find a place to pull over on the side of the road and I got out of the car, but I could barely control my legs. They were weak and trembling. I couldn't control my movements. It felt like my body was not my body, if that makes sense. I was throwing up nonstop, and my vision was getting blurry. Hyperventilating. Everything started to go black. It felt like my soul was going down this dark tunnel, and I couldn't even hear my family. I could just hear my own brain saying, "Oh, my god. Oh, my god."

The worst part about a panic attack is that the first time you experience it, you don't even *understand* you're having a panic attack.

I didn't know what in the world was happening to me—which made everything ten times scarier.

You start digging yourself deeper and deeper into the hole because you think you must literally be dying.

The only thing I could hear was my mom's voice. That was like the little ball of warmth in the darkness I was gravitating toward.

My mom just kept saying, "I just need you to come on back, OK?"

I don't even remember this because I was off somewhere else, but my mom said I just kept crying and repeating, "I disappointed everybody. I didn't do enough. I never do enough."

It was like I was spinning off somewhere in deep space, and the sound of her voice was pulling me back to earth. She just kept holding me, on the side of the road, in the puddle of my own puke, and saying, "It's gonna be fine. Just come on back to Momma. Come on back. Come on back."

I mean, all the love in the world to my dad, but there's just something about your mother's voice, you know?

She was my anchor. The warmth of her voice brought me back to earth, and I was finally able to calm down.

I remember when we got back home, my mom sat me down and just kind of looked at me in disbelief like, "Oh, my God, A'ja. Where did that come from? We had no idea. We thought you were *good*."

That's the thing about mental health that is so tricky.

On the outside, I *was* good. All the basketball fans out there might already have done the math in their heads. This happened four years ago? 2020?

Yes, 2020.

On the outside: Your girl was on fire. I had just made it to my first WNBA Finals. I won my first MVP trophy. I was getting my own custom colorways for my Nikes. I was on billboards. Shoot, I think I was a 94 overall in *NBA 2K*. Everybody was rocking with me. From the outside, it looked like I was on top of the world.

But on the inside, I was not OK.

Everything started after we lost to Seattle in the Finals. We had to stay in the WNBA bubble while we were playing, but once we lost, I ventured outside the Bubble for the first time in three months.

I know you understand because the whole world went through some version of it at the time, but that whole COVID Bubble experience was totally surreal. Like we were in some kind of science experiment. For months, we couldn't go anywhere. Couldn't do anything.

And for athletes, that meant no family. No friends. On FaceTime with my Aussiepoos, Ace and Deuce, every night, missing my babies. It really felt like we were all trapped.

The less I say about the accommodations, the better, because people out there had it a lot harder than us. But just to paint the picture, when we first arrived, they still had a mouse trap chilling right on the shelf in our laundry room. The showers wouldn't drain. Somebody found a *worm* chilling on the carpet in their room. Compared to the NBA's luxury Bubble at Disney World, it was Ratchet World.

So basketball became all-consuming. And that's a problem for me. Because just your ordinary baseline A'ja is obsessed with winning. But when you put A'ja in a Bubble for three months? It was like all my self-worth got channeled into one goal: winning that trophy.

It was so weird because our only window to the outside world was social media. We were experiencing all the turmoil and trauma through our phone screens. You had the ongoing tragedy of the pandemic, the BLM protests, the never-ending videos of police violence, and all the nasty rhetoric coming from the comment sections.

It felt like a disaster movie, and we were just viewing this *pain* and emotion from our little apartments in this fake, sunny, perfect little palm-tree paradise in Orlando.

You know how it was; it was like being sealed off in an alternate reality. So I kind of made myself *numb* to everything that was going on, just as a coping mechanism. It was like I wasn't fully processing the grief of it all. I was a basketball robot for the first time in my life.

When we got swept by Seattle in the Finals, to say I was devastated would be the understatement of the year. I put so much of the blame on myself. I felt like I had let everybody down. My teammates, my family, the fans, the organization. I felt like I just hadn't done enough. I felt like those whole three months in that place, in total isolation, not even being able to get a hug from my parents, was all for nothing. I just felt like such a failure.

I was just . . . empty.

When I finally got out of that Bubble and was back in the real world, it was like something *broke* inside me.

I'll never forget this one moment. It's such a random thing to have triggered my anxiety, but I was back at home in South Carolina, staying at my parents' house, and I was driving around for the first time in months. I went to get some fast food. Everything in that 2020 world was so strange if you weren't used to seeing it, you know? I pulled up to the restaurant, and everything inside was off-limits. They had changed the drive-thru line to have all the cashiers outside in their masks with an iPad to take your order, and I was SO BEFUDDLED. You had to roll down the window, and they would swipe your payment right there, and it was just so weird to me.

I was like, "Wait, this is what the world is like now? What else did I miss?"

I literally started getting this wave of anxiety as I was searching for my wallet. The world had changed while I was in my bubble, and I didn't know what was going on.

I was just so angry with myself. There were a lot of days when I couldn't get myself out of bed.

You didn't do enough. You didn't do enough. You didn't do enough.

You know how that cycle goes, right?

That anxiety gets up *on* you.

My decompression after the bubble led right into depression. Straight up. Capital D. Depressed. Not down. Not a little sad. Not "in my feelings." No. Depressed. But I didn't tell a soul. I kept everything from my family, even my parents, because I didn't want them to worry about me. As Black women, how many of us put on that mask every morning? Gotta be perfect! Gotta be smiling! Gotta be *strong*!

As Black women, it's like . . . weakness?

Weakness???

Don't even mention that word around me. We don't got *time* for that!!!

I witnessed it with my own mother when I was a kid. She could've had the hardest day at work, but when she came home at night, it was all smiles. It was all positive vibes. You would never catch her slipping. Never see her sweat.

How many of us fall into that same pattern? Personally, I have this vision for myself I feel I have to meet—not as a basketball player, but as a Black woman in America. As *A'ja Wilson*.

I feel I need to handle every situation with grace and poise and positivity. I can't let them catch me losing my cool, right?

Oh, you know A'ja is always gonna handle her business.

Don't worry about A'ja.

A'ja's good. She got this.

(Meanwhile, when the TV cameras are all gone, and I'm in bed by myself, I'm crying my eyes out.)

I can give all the advice I want in this book, but at the end of the day, I am a human being, just like you.

I am not perfect. Not even close.

If anything, I was trying to play this character of the

perfect athlete. The perfect role model. The perfect personality on social media. I was trying to wear all these different hats at once as a strong Black woman, and then, one day, when they all fell off my head, I had no idea *who* I was.

But you know what?

That panic attack was probably the best thing that ever happened to me. After that day, I couldn't pretend like nothing was wrong. I couldn't pretend like I was just pissed off that we had lost in the Finals.

Obviously, when you're throwing up on the side of the road in front of your whole family, it's not just about *basketball*. You got some other issues to unpack, girl.

I started letting my therapist in more. I started being more honest with my parents. I started being more real with *myself*. One of the things I realized was I had been holding on to a lot of pain and grief for a long time.

A big part of it was me not fully coming to terms with the death of my grandmother when I was in college. The last decade of my life has been a really wild ride—going to South Carolina, winning the national championship, getting drafted into the W, the Bubble season. When you're on that roller coaster, it can be hard to process *real* life, let alone real *loss*.

I can't really sum up what my grandmother meant to

me. It's impossible. In this book, I have tried my best, but some things can't be expressed in language. If only you could live inside my brain and feel a hug from Hattie Rakes. Then you would understand why it took me years to finally let her go.

I mean . . . losing someone like that . . . what can I say? I just wasn't able to process it. I buried the grief for years. In trying to make her proud, and live up to all her expectations for me, and carry on her legacy, I thought I had to be perfect.

When the bubble finally popped, and I felt like I had failed, and the world seemed to be going crazy all around us, all those emotions just came flooding out on the way to do some dang outlet shopping.

The WNBA MVP was on the side of the road, sobbing and thinking she had let everybody down.

Yes, I battled depression.

After an MVP season.

Yes, I had panic attacks.

After an MVP season.

That's not weakness. It's just *real*.

In the end, I *needed* to go through that. I had to come to terms with the complicated emotions I had buried for so long so I could grow as a person. And that's thanks to my psychiatrist, Dr. Casey.

I had to accept—no, no, no, I had to *embrace*—the fact that the *real* A'ja that I am on certain days isn't the same A'ja that a commentator sees, or that a teammate sees, or that even my best friend sees.

And that's OK.

My emotions are my emotions.

My pain is my pain.

My story is *my* story.

Listen, I can appreciate Kobe Bryant. I used to get myself all worked up watching his interviews on YouTube—driving myself crazy like, *You better get up at 5:00 a.m. and be in that gym before everybody else, A!!! MAMBA MENTALITY!!! WHILE THEY'RE SLEEPING, YOU'RE OUT HERE GRINDING!!!*

But you know what? Some mornings, I don't want to be that person. Some mornings, I want to sit in bed and cry my heart out a little bit and feel *all* the feelings. That's not a weakness. That's just how I cope with a little thing called life.

I refuse to feel guilty for being me. At the end of the day, there are different paths to greatness, and I feel like we don't hear that message enough, especially as Black women.

You can be vulnerable and still be the MVP.

You can be vulnerable and still be the CEO.

You can be vulnerable and still be in the White House.

You can be vulnerable and still get that promotion.

You can be vulnerable and still be an amazing mom.

You don't have to put the mask on every morning and pretend it's all good.

And listen, I am not judging. I *get it* if you choose to put that mask on some days. As Black women, there's so much pressure on us to be everything to everyone. We're expected to wear so many different hats and to juggle so many different roles—and to do it all with a smile. ('Cause you know what they're gonna label us if we don't, right??)

I swear, it's like we're always thinking so much about everybody else that we forget about ourselves. And then at the end of a long hard day, you climb onto that couch and put your feet up and scroll through the apps, and it's Validation Time. You better be getting that validation from the world through all those streams and apps and likes and comments, or what is your value?

Are you loved?

Are you respected?

Are you enough?

Well, let me just say this really loud, for anybody in the back of the room who needs to hear it today:

You are *enough*.

More than enough.

As a matter of fact, the best is yet to come.

Those are the exact words my grandmother used to tell me when I was a little girl. So simple. So powerful.

The best is yet to come.

You will climb out of that darkness like I climbed out of mine.

I don't have an easy answer for how to do it. I don't have a ten-step program. But I would say that step one is the simplest of all:

Talk to somebody.

That was how I got on the path to feeling like myself again. And a big part of it, for me, was to really turn back to my roots and understand that my place in this world is a lot bigger than what my job is, or how much money I got in my bank account, or how many trophies I got in my cabinet, or what the world thinks of me.

About four months after my panic attack, they had a ceremony to unveil my statue outside our arena at the University of South Carolina. To this day, I still cannot believe my crazy-ass second mom Dawn Staley convinced the administration to commission a bronze *statue* of me to commemorate the school's first national championship. When she first told me it was real, I said,

"Don't people usually gotta have one foot in the grave first? I'm twenty-four years old! Is this even legal?"

But hey, Dawn has the ultimate clout. So I guess when you make history, they make exceptions.

The best is yet to come.

I thought about those words on the day they unveiled that statue, and they took on such a deeper meaning. I was so nervous to give my speech. After coming out of such a dark few months, I was overwhelmed by the moment. I must have practiced my speech five or six times in front of my friends, and I was shaking in my heels.

But then I just kept thinking about what my grandmother would say if she could've been there to see it. And that's when everything clicked.

The statue . . . it's not about me.

It's about *us*.

It's about all the little girls who are going to walk across that campus over the next ten years, fifty years, one hundred years. Before long, they're probably not even going to remember the name A'ja Wilson. But they'll definitely remember the feeling of seeing a young Black woman immortalized in bronze on that campus. And that's such an important image for those girls to see—especially in the South.

I hope we do a good job of teaching those little girls

their history. In one hundred years, who knows what they'll think about the times we're living through. Who knows what they will remember? Will we be living in a better world by then? I really don't know.

But the truth is . . .

That young Black woman immortalized in bronze?

Her own *grandmother* wasn't allowed to step on that same campus when she was her age.

Her own *father* wasn't allowed to play basketball for that same university when he was her age.

And she *herself* had walked to middle school on streets named after slave owners, past houses that proudly flew the Confederate flag.

When I saw them unveil my statue, that was the wave that came crashing over me. Those were the memories that came flooding back. Not my games, not my buckets, not my career. No, no, no. My *history*.

I cried happy tears for the first time in a long time. It was like a voice came to me from the heavens. I could hear my grandmother telling me, "Honey, stop *crying*. What's there to cry about, anyway? You *know* the best is yet to come, right?"

I took a long deep breath. The weight came off. I felt like I'd been reborn.

That's my story. That's my truth.

It feels good just to say it.

Dang, it feels *good!*

And before I get up out of here—my only advice for you, if you're feeling like I was feeling? Please, just let it *out.*

Drop the mask for a minute and talk to somebody. A therapist, a friend, a family member, *somebody.*

There's nothing to feel embarrassed about. Puke in the car. Cry by the side of the road. Sob in the middle of your math class. Let it out. Who cares?

I guarantee you, whatever you are feeling, there is a solution. I promise you.

Stop trying to be perfect. Let the weight come off you. Lean on somebody *else* for a minute.

We got you.

Hey, we *got* you.

You are not alone.

The best is yet to come.

Your friend,

Aja Wil~

10

IF YOU CAN SEE HER,
YOU CAN BE HER

Dear Black Girls,

This one is for all the girls who are too cool to raise their hands and ask the question.

This is for all the girls who want to know my "secret."

This is for all the girls who want to know the cheat code to life.

Oh yes, I see you all out there. Anytime I do an event with one of my sponsors or at a basketball camp and there's a room full of girls, it's always the same scenario. Y'all are just trying to compete for who can seem the most *over it*, huh?

"Like, what are we even *doing* here, ohmygod."

You can't fool me because I've *been* you.

I'll never forget when I was the featured speaker at the 2023 McDonald's All American Games banquet. This is pretty much like the Oscars of the high school basketball world. It's what every kid dreams about. If you make McDonald's? You made it. You're really *her*.

So you would've thought the whole room would have been beaming, right?

Nope.

Room full of the most *over-it* girls you've ever seen in your life. Heads down. Phones out. Scrolling their lives away. I swear, you look out into a crowd of girls now, and 90 percent of those necks will be *hunched*.

Girls, for real, what is even *happening* on that phone? Am I missing something?

These girls were too cool for me. They were really on some *Gossip Girl* vibes. I actually started getting nervous backstage.

And what burned me up so much was how *fly* they all looked. Back in my day, they still made us wear formal dresses to the McDonald's banquet. They legit had the dress patrol coming around the room to make sure everyone was on point. We're talking about a room full of some of the best hoopers in the country, and everybody is on growth spurt number two or three, and they're making us wear dresses like it's prom? We don't got no money! We're seventeen! What do you think those fits were looking like?

Busted.

They set us up, I swear. Don't look at the pictures.

Fast forward to the 2023 banquet, and all these girls were wearing these dope bomber jackets. Jeans. Jordans. They even had a DJ! They're playing hip-hop like we're in the club!

I'm in full old-head mode, and I won't apologize for it. I'm like, "Do y'all even know how lucky you are?"

Nope. All the girls were hunched over their phones, tip-tappin' away, not even talking to one another.

I remember I was backstage talking to the emcee right before I was about to go on, and he said, "Make sure you leave enough time for a Q and A. When you get up there, those girls are going to ask you so many questions."

I'm looking at him like, *Sir, have you ever seen a real seventeen-year-old lately? It's going to be* crickets.

Sure enough, I get up on the stage and give my speech, trying to pour my heart out to these girls and get them engaged. I look out into the seats, all nervous . . .

Crickets. It's dead. Not even a little smile. You could've put the best stand-up comedian in the world in front of these girls, and they would have been looking at them like, *Huh? Who are you? Are you on TikTok?*

They had me *shook.*

"So, do y'all have any questions for me?"

Silence.

"Ask me anything."

Silence.

"Anything? Ha ha . . . Anything, y'all."

Finally, by the grace of God, one brave girl in the back of the room raised her hand. I could have run up and given her a hug. I was so relieved.

I said, "Yes? You, back there? What's up, girl?"

She asked, "Did you party in college?"

The whole *room* started cracking up.

I said, "Thank you so much for that question. Um."

I'm looking over at the emcee and all the McDonald's people like: "Can I be real or no? What's the protocol here?"

They're all looking at each other, *Uhhh.*

The seventeen-year-olds had 'em shook. But you know I'm always going to keep it unapologetic, so I said, "Yes, as a matter of fact, I *did* party in college."

Everyone's laughing. Now we got 'em loose!

"I can't lie to you. I enjoyed my college experience. Is there a video circulating out there of me falling off a table? It's possible. It's unconfirmed."

I had to give them the real me! These girls can spot a fake a mile away!

"Listen, the guys can go to college for one year and

then go to the NBA. You girls are going to be at that place for four full years. Embrace it to the fullest. And remember to hydrate."

You could see the whole room take an exhale like, *Wait a minute. She's normal? She's a human being?*

When I got off that stage, I got *swarmed*. I felt like Beyoncé. I had all these girls coming up to me like I was just their homegirl.

For the first time, they really *saw* me.

And if you can see her? You can be her.

They were firing off questions like:

"A'ja, did you have a boyfriend in college?"

"I had a *halfway* boyfriend. Drama, drama, drama."

"Have you ever gotten ghosted?"

"YES. Are you serious?"

"How many tattoos do you have?"

"Fifteen."

"Is training camp fun?"

"*Hell no,* it's not fun. It sucks! We have two-a-days every single day!"

"Do you fly first class?"

"Sometimes. And yes, I still get old white men cutting in front of me thinking I'm not *really* in the premium line. (Yes, I'm first class, *Robert*.)"

"How can I make it to the WNBA?"

"Work your ass off. But you *still* might not make it. So you better have a backup plan."

"How do you play in acrylics?"

"Like this. *Swish.*"

"How much money you make?"

"Not enough."

One of the girls who had been too cool for school just fifteen minutes before came right up to me like, "Ohmygod, A'ja Wilson. You are literally on my vision board in my bedroom."

That night with those girls made me realize two things:

One, I am old as dirt. I am actually on someone's vision board.

Two, all these girls see—24/7, all day, every day—on social media is a fake reality. They look at somebody like me—*me,* embarrassing A'ja, let alone somebody who really got it going on—as this superhero. It wasn't until we broke the ice, and they started asking me real questions, that they understood I was just like them. I had the same boy problems. I had the same drama. I had the same cringe-inducing moments. Wait, did I say *had?* I *have!* Present tense!

Everything on these girls' phones is straight PROPAGANDA. They see everyone's most perfect moments.

They see the world through a filter—literally. They see only what everyone else wants them to see, with all the blemishes and the ashy legs and the I'm-looking-an-absolute-mess-both-spiritually-and-physically days conveniently edited out.

You ever notice how everybody on Instagram got *money?*

Does it grow on trees?

And why is everyone always in *Paris?*

How do y'all keep permanently moisturized on that app?

It's a LIE.

So what do you think happens when these young women look in the mirror? How can they not feel bad about themselves? How can they not feel *less than?* How can they not start to feel depressed?

"Dang, everybody else got it all figured out and I'm just . . . *me.*"

It's like every single girl out there goes into this *so-over-it* posture that's almost like a defense mechanism.

We'll call it PSSSHHH MODE.

As in: *Pssshhh. I don't even care. Whatever.*

And I *get* it. I really do. I don't blame any of y'all for going full PSSSHHH MODE. But I know it's all just a way to cope with the world, and you wish you could be more vulnerable—more loose, more *you.*

When I talk to young women now, and they really get comfortable, it's so clear to me how desperately they want to achieve great things in life. But the problem is, they're conditioned by social media to look for the quick fix. The magic wand. Some kind of *secret.* It's like all those clickbait articles. "You won't believe this ONE WEIRD TRICK."

These girls want an answer, and they want it in six seconds or less.

They come up and say things like, "I want to be you. How did you do it? What's the secret?"

Girl, the secret is there *is no* secret. Everything that I have in my life, I have built up brick by brick. That is what this entire book is about. You were probably wondering: A'ja, we're at the end of this joint—where is all the self-help? Where're the tips? Where's my magic wand?

Shoot, life is tough, girl. Don't get a wand; get a helmet.

Every step along the way, I have failed. I have cried out eyelashes. I have walked off a ballet stage mid-performance. I have asked my parents to put me up for adoption. I have told Dawn Staley half a dozen different times, "I am definitely transferring! I hate this! I quit!"

Before I made history, I made a million mistakes. And I still do.

I wish more young women could see a real window into our lives and not just the curated Instagram squares that serve as our windows. If you really saw what we go through to achieve greatness, it wouldn't look pretty.

When we won the WNBA title in 2022, it might have seemed like we were this unstoppable team from the outside. But if you were behind the scenes with us, you would have seen a lot of bad days. I'll never forget the Becky Hammon Emergency Meeting. We got served up a piping-hot humble pie with a side of ice cream from the legend herself.

We were on a losing streak right before All-Star Weekend. We were getting *smacked* by teams we had no business even losing to. We were coasting! I can't lie! (What did I warn you about feeling yourself too much?) I go off to the All-Star Game in Chicago. I'm just trying to enjoy my weekend! Where're the parties? Immediately after the game, Coach Hammon calls me on the phone. "I need you on the 6:00 a.m. flight to New York. Team meeting."

Dang, Coach. You got me setting the 3:45 a.m. airport alarm??? OK.

I get to the team hotel in Manhattan, and we're all in this big conference room, like we're at an accounting conference. There's no game film set up. No whiteboard. None of the coaches are in the room yet, so we naturally start goofing off. My teammate Kelsey Plum had just won the MVP at All-Star, and it's the W, so this trophy was comically small.

"KP, this thing is smaller than my iPhone. This like a tee-ball trophy."

Everybody's laughing.

In comes Coach.

"What's so funny?"

Silence.

"Sorry, Coach. KP's trophy. It's . . . small."

"Oh, that's funny, huh? That's hilarious."

You could feel the mood of the room shift into: *Uh-oh. We in troubllllle.*

She went off. The media always loves it when a male coach goes off. Those clips are always going viral. But I wish they had more appreciation for when our female coaches go into ass-kicking mode, because they will BREAK YOU DOWN on a whole other level. She came for our souls.

I will not quote Coach directly, but her message was basically: You haven't *won* sh*t. You haven't *done* sh*t. And unless you change your frame of mind, you're not gonna *be* sh*t. You are pretenders. Period.

When I tell you it was a come-to-Jesus moment, it's not a figure of speech. She went biblical on us. We were getting hit with Old Testament quotes. She held us to account for being too cool for school. She held us to account for wanting to skip straight to the victory parade. She held us to account for having a runner-up mentality. A "we coulda did it" mentality.

Then she pulled a *brick* out of her briefcase.

(At least it looked exactly like a real brick. Turns out it was foam.)

She slammed it on the table and said, "This is us. We are going to do this. Brick by brick."

The game was simple. Every single time we got a win the rest of that season, we earned a brick. The goal was to build a house. Coach actually got the idea because her two young sons love to play as little construction men. She ordered, like, a hundred of those things on Amazon.

I can't lie to you; at first, we all thought it was the dumbest thing in the world. We were rolling our eyes the first week. (I'm sorry—we're the worst.)

But then a funny thing happened.

We turned our losing streak around and got the first few bricks. We built our foundation. And then it got really addicting. Any time we got a new brick, we would go *crazy*. It was like frat-house vibes. Straight to the locker room: "Where's the brick? *Brick! Brick! Brick!*"

When we lost and we didn't get that new brick? Oh, my gosh, we were legit crushed.

"Coach, we only lost by a bucket. The refs were crooked, I swear! We can't get a brick?"

"No. Bricks are for winners."

"Daaaaaaang, Coach."

If you didn't already guess, the point is not about the bricks. The point is you can turn a bunch of *so-over-it,* too-cool-for-school WNBA players into little kids again if you can tap in to something that is very hard to explain.

Maybe it's part of "the secret." Not just to basketball, but to life. And maybe that's why it's so hard to put into words.

My second mom, the great Dawn Staley, has a theory about it. She always says, "Great teams have a certain sound. They have a feeling. They have a vibe."

You can probably just put your ear up to the door of a locker room after a win, or especially after a loss, and you can *hear* the vibes of a great team. It sounds like our Vegas team after we won a tough game on the road, and everybody was dancing around chanting, "We want the brick! We want the brick!"

I can't tell you exactly what a winning team does in practice, or what protein shakes they drink, or what they do in the gym, because if it were that simple, everyone would copy it.

But I can tell you exactly what a winning team *sounds* like.

They're not calling each other out; they're calling each other in.

They're not pointing fingers; they're holding up their hands and saying, "That's on me. My bad."

They're taking more lessons from the losses than from the wins.

And they bought in to the grind of the journey and not just the champagne showers at the destination.

Because, trust me, even when you win a championship, it's 99 percent pain and 1 percent champagne.

There're no shortcuts. There's no magic wand. There's no weird trick.

Do you think I am just talking about basketball here?

What book you been reading, girl?

I am only twenty-seven years old, so I cannot pretend

to know all the secrets of the universe. (Hydrate? Exfoliate? I guess I know two.)

But if I have learned one underrated lesson from my own journey so far, it's that adversity is like fertilizer for greatness.

And for my Black girls out there, that's really good news for you because the world got a hell of a lot of fertilizer still stored up for y'all.

Every hard, scary, terrifying, embarrassing, or downright awful part of my life gave me some kind of new superpower.

I was dyslexic. I thought differently than everybody else. But I embraced my unique and unapologetic voice, and now I am fulfilling my childhood dream by writing this book. Bet some of my old teachers can't believe it.

I lost my grandmother—my best friend, my purpose, my *why*. But she gave me the greatest gift of all. The gift of hope. She has been that angel who has guided my entire life. I've learned just as much from her since she's passed as I did when she was still here.

I battled through depression and panic attacks. But I came out the other side with a much better understanding of my self-worth and what actually matters in life. (It certainly ain't money or trophies. Those are nice, but it's all about your *people*.)

And yes, I was a Black girl in a predominantly white school. When I got invited to The Infamous Birthday Party, I got told that I had to sleep outside because of my skin color. For a lot of people, that's a sob story. But you know what? I've grown to appreciate even *that* terrible memory.

I hope those girls enjoyed their cute little cupcakes back then while little A'ja was crying her eyes out. Because that naive Black girl grew up to be a strong Black woman who has lived her dreams.

I helped *build* the trophy case at South Carolina.

I got immortalized in bronze.

I won Olympic gold.

I started my own foundation for kids with dyslexia.

I did exactly what my grandma predicted.

I put a lot of pins where I've been.

I accomplished so many things that my fourth-grade self never would have imagined.

So you know what? Fourth grade can go to hell. I've been invited to a *lot* of dope parties since then, and we weren't drinking no apple juice.

As a matter of fact, I think the single best party I've ever been to in my life was the plane ride back home after we won the WNBA title. It brought every single thing in my life full circle. The team told us that our families could fly back with us on our private jet—and it was the first time my mom and dad had ever been on a PJ.

It was just a whole *scene*. It was a five-hour flight, so it got a little *litty* in that plane. Everyone was hugging, clinking glasses, and just having the time of our lives. The flight attendants kept coming around asking if anyone wanted food, and it blew my dad's mind.

He kept looking at my mom and saying, "What? They got hamburgers on this jet? *What?* Eva! Eva! They got *burgers* on this jet."

"I know, Roscoe; you told me ten times. You can't eat all the food! Act like you been here before!"

"Shoot, I only ever get peanuts and chips. This is *nice*."

He was in full Dad Mode.

He was chompin' on his burger, looking over at me like, *I'm so proud. All those nights in the gym. All those road trips.*

I said, "Remember when you told me I was *trash?*"

"You *were* trash. Look at you now."

I will remember that flight more than I will remember most of the buckets I scored that season. The point is not the trophy. The point is not basketball. The point is *my people*. Through thick and thin, they were always there for me. Two years after I was hunched over on the side of the road in South Carolina, having a panic attack, thinking

I was the world's biggest failure, we all got to have that moment together. That moment of: "We really did it."

Nobody even had to say it. We were all thinking it: Grandma would be so, so proud.

Black girls all around the world, I don't have a magic wand for you. I don't have the answers to all your questions. I am still figuring it out myself.

I don't know how to make the world hear us. I don't know how to make these boys behave. I don't know how to wear six different hats at once. I don't know how to be confident without being labeled a *bitch* or vulnerable without being labeled *emotional*.

I don't know how to be perfect.

But I can tell you one thing, Black girls.

Here's the real secret, passed down to me from my late, great, incomparable grandmother Hattie Rakes. It's the ultimate gift. And it's just three simple words we can never hear enough: I love you.

So Black girls,

I love you. This was for you.

Always,

Aja Wil~

ACKNOWLEDGMENTS

There are far too many people to thank for being a part of this story of my life. Y'all know who you are, and I love you.

But I want to especially shout out Alana Casner and Sean Conboy, for all the deep conversations; Jade-Li English, for always having my back (and my front and my side); my family, for being the best that anybody could ever ask for; my friends, for always keeping me grounded; Dawn Staley, for being a second mom to me; and my future children, who I hope will one day keep writing new chapters of this beautiful Wilson story.

P.S. Hey, Mom and Dad. I did it. Your girl is an author.

ABOUT THE AUTHOR

A'JA WILSON is an Olympic gold medalist and a two-time WNBA MVP currently playing for the Las Vegas Aces. Off the court, A'ja has built the A'ja Wilson Foundation, which serves as a resource for children who struggle with dyslexia and empowers them to reach their full potential. She resides in Las Vegas.

MOMENT
OF LIFT
BOOKS

Moment of Lift Books, created by Melinda
French Gates in partnership with Flatiron Books,
is an imprint dedicated to publishing original
nonfiction by visionaries working to unlock a
more equal world for women and girls.

To learn more about Moment of Lift Books,
visit www.momentoflift.com.